An Invincible Summer Within

An Invincible Summer Within

Contemplation Practice

Padraic O'Hare

CASCADE *Books* · Eugene, Oregon

AN INVINCIBLE SUMMER WITHIN
Contemplation Practice

Cascade Books
An Imprint of Wipf and Stock Publishers
199 W. 8th Ave., Suite 3
Eugene, OR 97401

www.wipfandstock.com

PAPERBACK ISBN: 978-1-6667-3065-4
HARDCOVER ISBN: 978-1-6667-2243-7
EBOOK ISBN: 978-1-6667-2244-4

Cataloguing-in-Publication data:

Names: O'Hare, Padraic, author.

Title: An invincible summer within : contemplation practice / by Padraic
O'Hare.

Description: Eugene, OR: Cascade Books, 2022 | Includes bibliographi-
cal references.

Identifiers: ISBN 978-1-6667-3065-4 (paperback) | ISBN 978-1-6667-
2243-7 (hardcover) | ISBN 978-1-6667-2244-4 (ebook)

Subjects: LCSH: Contemplation. | Meditation.

Classification: BV2091.C7 O37 2022 (print) | BV2091 (ebook)

09/30/22

Dedicated to
Brother Michel Bettigole, OSF (Gus), 1940–2017
A Franciscan

*"I think that he was the only person I have ever known
who was utterly incapable of being mean spirited."*
—Brother Owen Justinian Sadlier, OSF

In the midst of hate I found there was within in me, an invincible love. In the midst of tears, I found there was within me an invincible smile. In the midst of chaos, I found there was within me an invincible calm. I realized through it all, that . . . in the midst of Winter, I found there was within me an invincible Summer. And that makes me happy. For it says that no matter how hard the world pushes against me, within me there is something stronger, something better, pushing right back.

—Albert Camus

Like a Great Tree spread out over me
with love in every limb.

—Hildegard of Bingen

Contents

Precis

This book is for anyone who wants to be happy and good—beginners or "experts," religious believers or secular humanists. It is for young adults (the pious as well as the "nones"), and adults; for professors, campus ministers, dancers, carpenters, lawyers, plumbers, teachers, corporate workers, a sampling of the mix who show up every two years at the international Thomas Merton meetings. It is for use alone or in circles of contemplation (meditation) practitioners.

To be happy and good, a person needs to acquire (slowly, patiently, gently) over the course of their lives the skill set of regular access to their inner lives, where their true, distinct from false, self resides in a great landscape of stillness, simplicity, and presence, listening, awake, mindful. This regular access is encounter with a Source within us that mitigates fear, regret, anxiety, anger, pain, chaos, and resentment! The person who engages in this practice grows good and happy, or better and more happy! Or, if they live with great suffering, less sorrowful. This practice is called contemplation practice.

The word *expert*, in the phrase "beginner or 'expert,'" is in quotes purposely. Experts are finished growing. Always be a beginner!

Preface: Contemplation and COVID

When the contemplation (meditation) practice circle with whom I have joined almost every Monday for about twenty years resumed meeting after an eighteen-month layoff for the plague, Sheila J. Trieff, a clinical social worker and one of three facilitators, led our practice. This is how she began the practice.

Meditation for Return

This moment is a balm for my soul, seeing each one of you, seeing your eyes, being in your presence.

For months (and months!) I have summoned you up in my mind.

For now, we are here together.

These pandemic times have brought with them so many feelings and explorations.

I have felt loss and anger and distraction. I have been confused and disoriented.

And I have also had the opportunity to reach inside in a deep way, to investigate thoughts, values and, yes, closets.

Perhaps we all share these experiences.

As in meditation, these disturbances and interruptions are normal, and when we set our intentions we are invited *not* to start over, but to begin again.

So let us begin again, my friends.

Breathing in love,

Breathing out peace.

We are home.

Acknowledgments—Thomas Merton and Others

Diarmaid MacCulloch, the church historian, coined the phrase "the democratization of spiritual exploration," that all may seek holiness, in his book *Silence: A Christian History* (2013). He writes of Merton and this movement, "It is always dangerous to take an individual as symbolic of any major shift in historical development, but the life of the monk, Thomas Merton (1915–68) offers a very tempting example." Richard Rohr says on camera of Merton, that he "almost reintroduced the word 'contemplation'" (DVD, *The Many Stories and Last Day of Thomas Merton*, Morgan Atkinson, 2015). And on September 24, 2015, before the United States Congress, Pope Francis, picking Merton and only three other United States citizens as exemplars, said "Merton was above all a man of prayer, a thinker who challenged the certitudes of his time and opened new horizons for souls and for the Church. He was also a man of dialogue, a promoter of peace between peoples and religions."

This book is dedicated to the wittiest person I've ever known. But its principle inspiration is "Uncle Louie" (Thomas Merton), who along with his best friend, Bob Lax, never lost his "child mind," and considered it "the only mind worth having."

For close to twenty years at this writing, I've sat in contemplative (meditative) practice every Monday morning with an admirable body of women and men, for whom I give profound thanks. Participants who continue to be active at this writing are marked with an "A" after their names. Elaine Demers (A), Lucy Gallagher (A), Mark Gallagher (A), Ruth Gannon (RIP), Eleanor Lyons (A), Donna Nutile (RIP), Claire Paulson (A), Donna Ricci, who first brought us together, Rebecca Taylor (A), Helen

Twomey (A), Sheila J. Trieff (A), Nancy B. Wright (A), and Peter Wyatt (A). Rebecca Taylor and Sheila Trieff conduct meditation with me, and samples of the richness they bring to enabling contemplation (meditation) appear in this text.

Thanks to beloved friends who take the inner life with utter seriousness, without however themselves turning solemn (a distinction owed to Russell Baker): James Carroll, Joel Emerson, Thomas H. Groome, Joseph Kelley, Howard Mandel, Doc Miller, Mary Minifie, Scott Ness, and John Rowan. Finally, and most profoundly, thanks to my immediate family Bucky and Meghan, five-year-old Sammy, and my wife, Peggy.

Introduction

Contemplation

Here is collected thirty years of guided meditations conducted by me, engaged with Jews, Christians , Muslims, Buddhists, Hindus, and secular humanists, sometimes such a mix sitting side by side; with children, teens, young adults (many of them "nones"), aged adults, graduate students, professionals engaged in healing service with especially wounded people, and with friends.

These experiences have convinced me of three things. The first is that this practice is for unity, practice to become one with . . . with what? For the humanist Albert Einstein, one with the "profoundest reason [sometimes translated "the Highest Wisdom"] and the most radiant beauty which are only accessible to our reason in their most elementary forms—it is this knowledge and this emotion that constitutes the truly religious attitude. . . . Enough for me the mystery of the eternity of life, and the inkling of the marvelous structure of reality."[1]

For the theist, Augustine of Hippo:

> What is it that I love when I love you? . . . A kind of light, a kind of voice, a certain fragrance, and an embrace, when I love my God: a light, voice, fragrance, food and embrace of my inmost self, where something limited to no place shines into my mind, where something not snatched away by passing time sings for me, where something no breath blows away yields to me its scent, where there is savor undiminished by famished eating, and where I am clasped into a union of which

1. Einstein, *World as I See It*, 16.

no satiety can tear me away. This is what I love when I love my God.[2]

The second conviction is that success in this practice is measured by the extent to which those who engage in it in a sustained way grow more *still, simple,* and *present,* really mindful or possessing mindfulness, *Sati,* in Pali—a human quality currently taking a terrible beating in the hands of contemporary meditation dilettantes.

In his Fragment 29, Meister Eckhart says that nothing is more like God than stillness. In the second volume of his journals, Thomas Merton asks "if the Risen Christ would always shine in my heart and all around me and before me in his Easter simplicity."[3] Thich Nhat Hanh, rescuing the practice of the present or mindfulness, says, "When we are mindful touching deeply the present moment, we can see and listen deeply, and the fruits are always understanding, acceptance and the desire to relieve suffering and bring joy . . . .To me mindfulness is very much like the Holy Spirit. Both are agents of healing."[4]

But, reader beware. The enemy of contemplative (meditative) being is striving for success. The Tibetan Buddhist master Pema Chodron addresses this essential insight for practice:

> Meditation is about seeing clearly the body that we have, the mind that we have, the domestic situation that we have, the job that we have, and the people who are in our lives. It's about seeing how we react to all these things. It's seeing our emotions and thoughts just as they are right now, in this very moment, in this very room, on this very seat. It's about not trying to make them go away, not trying to become better than we are, but just seeing clearly with precision and gentleness . . . . The desire to change is fundamentally a form of aggression toward yourself."[5]

2. Kelley, *Saint Augustine of Hippo,* 77.

3. Cited in Montaldo, *Year with Thomas Merton,* 100.

4. Hanh, *Living Buddha, Living Christ,* 14.

5. Chodron, *Wisdom of No Escape,* 14.

Stillness, simplicity, and mindfulness—practicing to be present and to listen—the qualities that constitute "success" in being contemplative, these very qualities assist the practitioner to resist practicing for success! These elements—stillness, simplicity, and mindfulness—are underlined in one of the several versions of the common Buddhist lesson that Tao is everyday mind, and everyday mind is this: when one is tired one should sleep, and hungry, one should eat. Stillness, simplicity, and mindfulness are also underlined in the whimsical "definition" of himself ascribed to Merton that what he does is live, how he prays is breath, and what he wears is pants.

The third conviction my years engaged in contemplation education and practice leaves me with is best expressed by a quote which appears in an essay by Nicholas Kristof entitled "What Religion Would Jesus Belong To?" Here Kristof quotes Brian D. McLaren:

> What would it mean for Christians to rediscover their faith not as a problematic system of beliefs, but as a just and generous way of life, rooted in *contemplation* and expressed in *compassion?* (Italics added.)[6]

The spiritual life is unquestionably "enter[ing] the darkness of interior renunciation . . . ," (Merton),[7] the discipline practiced by both the religious and the humanist, of renouncing the false self and becoming a real or true self. But this discipline of contemplation (meditation) is the premier social act as well and the furthest thing from flight. The contemplative person renounces flight and rushes toward the sister, the brother, the one in need of compassion, mercy, justice, forgiveness. They also seek beauty in the lives of sisters and brothers.

Nowhere is the link between contemplation and compassion more powerfully expressed than in the words of Gustavo Gutierrez. (He employs the word "practice," practice being part of "God's plan for history," for compassion.) He writes:

6. Kristof, "What Religion Would Jesus Be?"
7. Merton, *New Seeds,* 157.

Contemplation and practice together make up the *first act*; theologizing is the *second act*. We must first establish ourselves on the terrain of spirituality and practice; only subsequently is it possible to formulate discourse on God in an authentic and respectful way. Theologizing done without the mediation of contemplation and practice does not meet the requirements of the God of the Bible. The mystery of life comes to life in contemplation and in the practice of God's plan for history; only in the second phase can this life inspire appropriate reasoning. . . . In view of this we can say that the first moment is *silence* and the second is *speech*.[8]

This third conviction requires further consideration. Much Western meditative practice employing Eastern technique is rightly criticized as simply another self-help regime and quite narcissistic.[9] Whereas, the years of practice I am evoking here, wherever and with whoever it has worked, have been an encounter with love, and as such the furthest thing from selfish self-centeredness. Thomas Merton assists this further consideration.

There is real and false contemplation (meditation) practice. Both induce what is experienced as peace. The false kind is the peace of flight from engagement, flight from the sister and brother, flight from problems, not manufactured ones, but problems the human good requires we face. The opposite of peace is not war but fear, the opposite of fear freedom. Therefore, peace is freedom. Freedom for the self-centered is the freedom of flight. Merton describes the state of heart for the authentic contemplative: "The only true joy in life is to escape the prison of our own false self and enter by Love into the Life Who lives and sings in the essence of every creature, in the core of one's own soul."[10]

The premier social virtue, the human strength to run toward rather than flee the sister and the brother, especially those who are suffering, is humility, a word which shares Latin roots with the words "human," "humor," and "dirt"! Humility allows a man or

8. Gutierrez, *On Job*, xiii.

9. For example, Young, "Brief Mindfulness Training."

10. Merton, *New Seeds*, 27.

woman to forget themselves on purpose, not in a self-abnegating way but in a wholesome and freeing way. Again Merton: "Contemplation should not be exaggerated, distorted, or made to seem great. It is essentially simply and humble. No one can enter into it except by the path of obscurity and self-forgetfulness."[11]

Merton says contemplation heals wounds that block simple kindness and fairness, what everyone is owed, what the Catholic Social Teachings call "commutative justice." Contemplation frees us from "collective thinking," thinking easily manipulated into hatred of groups, freedom these teachings call "social justice":

> All men [and women] seek peace first of all within themselves. . . . We have to learn to commune with ourselves before we can communicate with other men [and women] and with God. A [person] who is not at peace with [themselves] necessarily projects [their] interior fighting into the society of those [they live] with, and [spreads] a contagion of conflict all around [themselves].[12]

Those familiar with Merton's work will know he ceaselessly links discovering one's true or real self through contemplation practice with resisting "collective thinking," the "collectivity." Here is his chilling estimate of the manipulated person, the person with no inner life or a false inner life:

> You have needs but if you behave and conform you can participate in the collective power. You can then satisfy all your needs. Meanwhile in order to increase its power over you, the collectivity increases your needs. It also tightens its demand for conformity. Thus you become all the more committed to the collective illusion in proportion to becoming more hopelessly mortgaged to collective power.[13]

The contemplative person is increasingly compassionate, still, simple, and mindful, striving gently for integrity, for alignment

---

11. Merton, *Inner Experience,* 116.

12. Merton, *No Man Is an Island,* 126.

13. Merton, "Rain and the Rhinoceros," 16.

with the Real, unity with the Source experienced and articulated religiously or humanistically. A mystic! Evelyn Underhill writes: "Mysticism is the art of union with Reality. The mystic is a person who has attained that union in a greater or lesser degree, or who aims at and believes in such attainment."[14]

Practice

This book is designed to be used by individuals and groups. The author employs it both ways.

Some of the groups with whom I have practiced over the years sit on Japanese meditation pillows (*zafus*), some cross-legged, some in the semi-lotus position, the rare elastic practitioner in the full lotus. Many simply sit comfortably on chairs, backs straight, hands gently composed. The author practices sitting cross-legged on a bench.

As the reader will see, the bell (call it the Bell of Mindfulness if you like) is ubiquitous. By myself and in group settings, I employ a gong which is nineteen inches in circumference and six inches in diameter. Though distributed across the world, bells, pillows, mats, and other meditation aids and Zen garden decorations are available through DarmaCrafts, for many years located in Lawrence, Massachusetts, ten minutes from where I taught from 1988 until Spring 2018; now it is located in Fall River, Massachusetts.

For many years, I employed gentle, meditative music (for example Steve Halperin, David Ison, Tony Scott) for intervals between spoken elements of the guided meditation. Older, more mature persons and practitioners often prefer total silence between well-spaced verbal expressions in sayings, prayer-poems, *gatha* in Sanskrit, and bell intonations. Experiment and be flexible. I sometime employ *mantras* , here introduced in Session 21, and counting one's breath, introduced in Session 3.

The closest thing to "dogma" in what follows is that every session, as far as possible, begin with an exercise reminding practitioners to attend to their breathing. From Theophilus of Antioch

14. Underhill, *Practical Mysticism*, 10.

in the second century insisting that God's breath vibrates in ours, through to David Steindl-Rast in the twenty-first century stating that we are alive with God's breath, this has been central. And, of course, it is the centerpiece of Buddhist practice. Shunryu Suzuki says, "Moment by moment to watch your breathing, to watch your posture, this is true nature."[15]

The Manner of This Book

Two important points about my method in framing these meditations that I think the reader will find helpful. First, I do not hesitate to paraphrase writers whose wisdom finds its way into the spoken content of guided meditations. I do this to render spoken *gatha* clearer, more useful, and, at times, in my estimation, more beautiful. For example, the reader will first come across words from Shunryu Suzuki's *Zen Mind, Beginner's Mind* in Session 3: "You cannot find Buddha mind or Christ mind through arduous effort. Reality cannot be captured by thinking and feeling mind. Moment after moment to watch your breathing, to watch your posture is true nature."[16] For beauty or least to eliminate an unattractive word I've changed Suzuki's actual words, "You cannot find Buddha mind by *vivisection* ... ," to " through arduous effort." (Billy Collins admits that in his wonderful, playful, and moving poem "The Lanyard," he changed the venue of where he went to camp as a lad from the Catskills to the Adirondacks, because he thought the latter word more felicitous.)

A second example of paraphrase comes from Session 7, a session entirely composed of the religious songs of Kabir, the fourteenth-century Indian mystic and poet claimed by both Muslims and Hindus. In the excerpts from Kabir's ecstatic writing, the higher—and also deeper—power is variously referred to as "God," "He," "true Guru," "true Name *Om*," and "Formless One." I employ most of these, but do not use "God" or "He." This is because of a commitment to inclusion—masculine references are

15. Suzuki, *Zen Mind,* 135.
16. Suzuki, *Zen Mind,* 134–35.

rendered inclusive for all sources—and so that humanists who are not also materialists find the session beneficial. This also motivates me to sometimes paraphrase by putting "Buddha" in the text where the author does not, because so many humanists seem comfortable with Buddhist practice assuming that in Zen expression there is no God in Buddhism.

I don't employ ellipses in the "Sessions" section of this book. Also, there are no footnotes except for this introductory essay. The reason is that this is a book of practice employing ideas for practice, not a book about the ideas themselves. The reader who wishes to trace sources can refer to a unique bibliographic element employed here, called "Sources Employed in Sessions," in the Table of Contents. The initials of the book, tape, or film cited in a session appear right after the quote in the body of the meditation session. The full title of the books, tapes and films, arranged alphabetically according to these initials, and the author's name appear in this "Sources Employed in Sessions." For example, the first entry is *ADP, Abandonment to Divine Providence,* by Jean-Pierre de Cassaude, SJ.

This is a good point at which to say something about the bow and its place in practice. I do not propose lengthening the preliminary orientation speech at the beginning of Session 1 by speaking of the bow. But in my own solitary practice, as well as circles of practitioners, I often begin practice with a bow and invite members of the circle to do so. In *Zen Mind, Beginner's Mind* Shunryu Suzuki says the practitioner must always be ready to bow even at the time of death. In this he elevates the bow to the reverential place of the *S'hema,* the exhortation the rabbis tell us the faithful Jew should recite every day, and even at the time of death: *S'hema Israel Adoni elohenu, Adoni, echod;* "Hear Oh Israel, the Holy One, your God, your God is one."

In my own practice, I bow regularly, sometimes sitting on my bench, sometimes standing in front of the bench prior to sitting. When I do bow it is always a threefold bow, "saying," "I am bowing to let go of craving, rage, ignorance, pride, stubborn view, doubt, attachment, jealousy, and selfishness." "I am bowing to embrace the

gifts and the fruits of the Spirit. The gifts are the Spirit of knowledge, understanding, and wisdom, counsel, fortitude, piety (rever-
ence), and fear (awe) of the Lord (Isa 11:2f). The fruits are love,
joy, peace; patience, kindness, generosity; faithfulness, gentleness,
self control" (Gal 5:22–23). And then the third bow: "I am bowing in gratefulness." The vices which accompany the first bow are
called *samyojana*, knots of forgetfulness of being, and are rendered
variously in various Buddhist sources. Regarding the third bow,
consult Session 8 for more on gratefulness.

Some Special Features of This Book

I am proud of two gifts I think this book provides readers. The
first is an especially broad range of resources for the spiritual
life. An especially large "cloud of witnesses" is made available to
the reader who allows the book into their practice of trying to
live well. To pick a number randomly, the first fifteen sessions
contain passages from twenty-eight persons, in several instances
from more than one of their works. In order of sessions, these are
Thich Nhat Hanh, Chuang Tzu, Annabel Laity, Pema Chodron,
Thomas Merton, Robert Kennedy, SJ, Meister Eckhart, Shunryu
Suzuki, Henri Le Saux, OSB (Abishiktananda), Martin Laird,
OSA, Francis de Sales, Kabir, Saint Athanasius, the author(s) of
Ecclesiastes, the author(s) of Job, the author(s) of Lamentations,
James Finley, Thomas à Kempis, Catherine of Genoa, Blaise Pas-
cal, Karl Rahner, Gabriel Moran, Yves Bonnefoy, Parker Palmer,
John Climacus, Hesychius, Nicephorus the Solitary, and the au-
thor of *The Cloud of Unknowing*.

The second thing I think is unique about this book is its
profoundly interreligious character. I mean taking account of
humanist spirituality, acknowledging the qualitatively "religious"
character of humanisms that are not materialist, and framing a
lot of sessions so that, *with a little imagination, creativity, flexibility, and an experimental mentality*, a humanist who experiences Something More (like Einstein) can benefit personally and
with others from what's in the book. In this I am following an

instinct with me for many years, a genuinely healthy Catholic instinct that led me as a young man to choose as a subject for a doctoral thesis in the early 1970s the life and work of the great "religious humanist" Henry Nelson Wieman, a signatory of the first *Humanist Manifesto*. This instinct is supported by Pope Francis's early, felicitous, and continuing conversations with Italy's foremost humanist thinker, Eugenio Scalfari.[17] In this I am guided by Ronald Dworkin's *Religion without God*. He writes: "religion is deeper than God. Religion is a deep, distinctive and comprehensive worldview. It hold that inherent, objective value permeates everything, that the universe and its creatures are awe-inspiring, that human life has purpose and the universe order. A belief in God is only one manifestation of that worldview."[18]

Kinds of Practice in These Meditations

The sessions in this book are numbered. Except where noted, for example sessions on or around the occasions of Christmas and Easter, most sessions can be adapted for use by individuals or groups who are in religions (hereafter "religious" despite the reference to Dworkin) and who are humanist. Again, this requires imagination, creativity, flexibility, and experimentation.

Three crucial principles should guide the religious and the and humanists sculpting sessions. Sessions need not speak of God to be useful for the practice of religious people. The theist, of whatever stripe, needs merely to introduce God, the Divine, the Source, the Present One, the Holy One, etc. where they deem appropriate for themselves or a circle of practitioners with whom they are practicing. Throughout the history of Christianity the idea, and the feeling, that God is *Pure Being* lives richly alongside the experience that being one with Christ is being one with God. Readers familiar with Thomas Merton and *The Seven Story Mountain* will recall him discovering this, and feeling that theological Catholicism might be intellectually coherent, reading Etienne Gilson's *The*

17. Pope Francis, "Letter to a Non-Believer," September 4, 2013.

18. Dworkin, *Religion without God*, 1.

Spirit of Medieval Philosophy on the Long Island Rail Road headed for Douglaston, Long Island. They will also recall his rage, prompting him to think of throwing the book out the window of the train, when he saw "*imprimatur*" in the front of the book. That we need not name God to love God gets a boost from Saint Augustine's words "If you have grasped it, it is not God" (Sermon 117).

The second principle for humanists using the book is the reverse of the advice given above. The presence of the word *God*, or any name for an underlying, grounding, and overarching, transcendent source of value does not disqualify a session being employed by humanists *provided they are not also materialists.*

The third principle, noted already, for religious and humanist persons who employ the text: *be imaginative, creative, flexible, and experimental.*

Flexibility points both users to react creatively rather than defensively if a session employs words for deity and if it does not. Both flexibility and experimentation invite people employing this book to simply take things out and put things in if most of what they find in a particular session appeals to them. For the religious and for spiritual humanists alike there is also this: a great treasure of beautiful and universal metaphors for the Source. "God is breath" (Maximus the Confessor), "God is friendship" (Aelred of Rievaulx), "Like a great tree spread out over me with love in every limb" (Hildegard of Bingen), "The soul's center" (John of the Cross), "A Hidden Wholeness," (Thomas Merton), "My me," (Catherine of Genoa), "Love," (John the Apostle), the "Silent Infinite" (Karl Rahner), and on and on. The mystics in all the world's religions rarely call God "God." But the "God" their speech points to is always the God, as Rabbi Heschel writes, that demands action: "Religion as an institution, the Temple as an ultimate end, or, in other words religion for religions' sake, is idolatry. . . . The human side of religion, its creeds, rituals and instructions, is a way rather than a goal. The goal is 'to do justice, to love mercy and to walk humbly *with* [Heschel's emphasis] thy God.'"[19]

19. Heschel, *I Asked,* 40f.

Themes/Authors of Sessions

All sessions are intended to deal directly or indirectly with unity, stillness, simplicity, and presence, that is mindfulness or being awake. Some sessions derive their *gatha* entirely or almost entirely from one source, and some deal with a specific theme. In some cases a person or theme is mentioned in a given session but is pervasive throughout the book. Examples include emptiness, purity of heart, the Buddha, Thomas Merton, and the influence of Augustine. Examples of one-source and one-theme sessions include Meister Eckhart (4), Kabir (7), Abhishiktananda, Dom Henri Le Saux, OSB, (9), *The Rule of Benedict* (13), Christmas (16), the poetry of Mary Oliver (25, 26), Easter (29), Al Hallaj (35), Thomas Merton (30–34 and 69), Thomas Keating (54), Joan Chittister (60, 61), Saint Augustine (37), beauty (39), Robert Lax (46), salvation (47), emptiness (48), Saint Francis of Assisi (50), Evelyn Underhill (72), Buddha (51, 58, 59), the Sermon on the Mount (56), play (17, 57), gazing (62), time (63), suffering and anger (20), heart (45), and spring (50). And, as noted below, there is a mixing and matching of elements of Sessions 47 and 25 for a Pentecost session.

Mixing, Matching, Abbreviating, and Multiplying Sessions

The flexible and creative will find here not the seventy-two sessions the book seems to contain, but certainly a hundred, perhaps more. Most sessions have a considerable number of words, elements of "guidedness," *gatha* (prayer-poems), excerpts, sayings. These are for calling us back from distraction to gentle, persistent, patient focus on breathing, and then on nothing. But silences, lots fewer words, are for cultivating silence, stillness itself. Strike a balance in your technique between these two values: drop some *gatha* and lengthen the periods of silence. Sometimes try "speaking" at the beginning and the end only. Turn two sessions into four!

On "mixing and matching," the advice translates to *"Don't be slavish about following the order of each session."* For example, I sit with a group that tops out at ten when everyone shows. We meet for a half hour every Monday morning. Three of us guide practice. One Monday, right after Pentecost, I was facilitating practice, and I mixed and matched thusly: the beginning and ending of the session was taken from Session 47, and in the middle I read the poem by Mary Oliver, which is Session 25.

Mixing and matching, shortening and thereby multiplying, is also advised for always trying to begin each session with attention to mindful breathing, conscious breathing. I myself employ *gathas* more than once.

Sisters and brothers, I wish you good meditation.

Sources Employed in Sessions

ADP	*Abandonment to Divine Providence,* Jean-Pierre de Caussade, SJ. (Cited by Thomas Merton in a talk to young monks in 1966, recorded on a tape entitled *Solitude: Breaking the Heart*).
AIL	*An Interrupted Life,* Etty Hillsum.
AJ	*Asian Journal,* Thomas Merton.
AL	*Aurora Leigh,* Elizabeth Barrett Browning.
AMPD	*A Most Profitable Discourse etc.* Nicephorus the Solitary, cited in *ISL.*
ASA	*A Sunlit Absence: Silence, Awareness, and Contemplation,* Martin Laird, OSA
AWFCF	*Anger: Wisdom for Cooling the Flames,* Thich Nhat Hanh.
AYWTM	*A Year with Thomas Merton.* Edited and compiled by Jonathan Montaldo.
BG	*Bhagavad Gita.*
BK	*The Brothers Karamazov,* Fyodor Dostoyevsky. (Words given to Father Zossima.)
BKCBCOA	*Buddha's Kitchen: Cooking, Being Cooked, and Other Adventures in a Meditation Center,* Kimberly Snow. (The poem cited in this book is "What Breathes Us" by Leo Stein. The second and third stanzas appear in Sessions 41 and 42.)
BL	*The Blossoming of the Lotus,* Thich Nhat Hanh.
BP	*Being Peace,* Thich Nhat Hanh.

BYAA *Breathe, You Are Alive!,* Thich Nhat Hanh. (Cited in its own text as well as the opening poem, of the same title as the book, by Annabel Laity.)

C *Catholicism,* Richard P. McBrien. (Quoting Karl Rahner, SJ.)

CB *Celtic Benediction: Morning and Night Prayer,* J. Philip Newell.

CGB *Conjectures of a Guilty Bystander,* Thomas Merton.

CJD *The Crest Jewel of Discrimination,* Shankara. (Quoted in *HWFAGC.*)

CMTLLTA *Christian Mystics: Their Lives and Legacies Throughout the Ages,* Ursula King. (Quoting Pierre Teilhard de Chardin, SJ.)

CP *Contemplative Prayer,* Thomas Merton.

CPB *Christian Prayer: The Breviary.* (First and second antiphons for Christmas morning.)

CPPK *Collected Poems,* Patrick Kavanagh. "The Great Hunger."

CSA *Confessions of Saint Augustine,* Augustine.

CU *The Cloud of Unknowing,* Anonymous.

CWA *Contemplation in a World of Action,* Thomas Merton.

D *The Dhammapada.* Translated by the Pali.

DQ *Disputed Questions,* Thomas Merton.

DTW *Deeper than Words: Living the Apostle's Creed,* David Steindl-Rast, OSB.

DW *Dream Work,* Mary Oliver.

EWS *Encounters with Silence,* Karl Rahner, SJ.

FCP *Foundation for Centering Prayer,* Thomas Keating.

FMT *The Fourteen Mindfulness Trainings,* Thich Nhat Hanh.

GG   "God's Grandeur," poem by Gerard Manley Hopkins, SJ.

HGL   *The Hidden Ground of Love,* Thomas Merton.

HBSTM   "How Beauty Saved Thomas Merton," website on Maximus the Confessor.

HU   *The Heart of Understanding,* Thich Nhat Hanh. (This is the title of Thich Nhat Hanh's translation and commentary on the *Prajna Paramita Sutra,* the Buddha's teaching on emptiness).

HWFAGC   *Hindu Wisdom for All God's Children,* Francis X. Clooney, SJ.

IAW   *I Asked for Wonder,* Abraham J. Heschel, edited by Samuel T. Dresner.

IGP   *In God's Presence: Centering Experiences for Circles and Solitudes,* William Cleary.

IM   *The Intimate Merton: His Life from His Journals,* edited by William Shannon and Christine Boucher.

ISL   *Into the Silent Land,* Martin Laird, OSA.

IC   *Imitation of Christ,* Thomas à Kempis.

LBLC   *Living Buddha, Living Christ,* Thich Nhat Hanh.

LDA   *Ladder of Divine Ascent,* Saint John Climacus.

LL   *Learning to Love: Exploring Solitude and Freedom, Journal* vol. 6, Thomas Merton.

LYP   *Letters to a Young Poet,* Rainer Maria Rilke.

M   *Mysticism,* Evelyn Underhill.

MA   *Muqatta'at,* Al-Hallaj.

MAP   *Man at Play,* Hugo Rahner. (Quoting Thomas Aquinas.)

MEBH   *Meister Eckhart's Book of the Heart: Meditations for the Restless Soul,* Jon M. Sweeney and Mark S. Burrows. (What Sweeney and Burrows do here is much akin to what Merton did in *The Way of Chuang Tzu:* free translation, genuinely the thought and feeling of Eckhart and Chuang Tzu, but translated for contemporary times, creatively but faithfully.)

MEMT	*Meister Eckhart: A Modern Translation.* Translated by Raymond Blakney.
ML	*Morning Light: The Spiritual Journal of Jean Sulivan.*
MM	*The Miracle of Mindfulness,* Thich Nhat Hanh.
MPN	*Merton's Palace of Nowhere,* James Finley.
MTOW	*More Than One Way? Four Views of Salvation in a Pluralist World,* edited by Dennis Okholm and Timothy R. Phillips. (Quote is from "A Pluralist View," by John Hick.)
NLS	*No Ladder to the Sky,* Gabriel Moran.
NMI	*No Man Is an Island,* Thomas Merton.
NP	"The Nine Prayers," Thich Nhat Hanh. In *Contemplative Prayer,* Thomas Merton.
NSC	*New Seeds of Contemplation,* Thomas Merton.
NYT	*The New York Times,* William Gimes (obituary of Yves Bonnefoy, July 5, 2016).
OAL	*Our Appointments with Life,* Thich Nhat Hanh.
OJGTSI	*On Job: God-Talk and the Suffering of the Innocent,* Gustavo Gutierrez.
OMWH	*The Only Mind Worth Having: Thomas Merton and the Child Mind,* Fiona Gardner.
OW-P	*On Watchfulness,* John Climacus. Cited in *The Philokalia.*
P	*Pensées,* Blaise Pascal.
PA	*Pure Act: The Uncommon Life of Robert Lax,* Michael McGregore.
PHC	*Purity of Heart and Contemplation: A Monastic Dialogue Between Christian and Asian Traditions,* edited by Bruno Barnhart and Joseph Wong.

PP   *The Practice of Peace,* Thich Nhat Hanh. DVD.

RB   *The Rule of Benedict.* Edited by Timothy Fry, OSB.

RTC   *Reclaiming the Connection: A Spirituality of Connect-
            edness,* Kathleen Fischer.

RW   *The Religions of the World,* Huston Smith.

SCAAE   *Saccidananda: A Christian Approach to Advatic Expe-
            rience,* Abhishiktananda (Henri Le Saux, OSB).

S21stC   *Spirituality for the 21st Century: The Rule of
            Benedict,* Joan Chittister.

SE   *Spiritual Exercises,* Ignatius of Loyola.

SF   *Spirit of Fire: The Life and Vision of Teilhard
            de Chardin,* Ursula King.

SGH   *The Saints' Guide to Happiness,* Robert Ellsberg.

SHC   *Silence and Honey Cakes: The Wisdom of the Desert,*
            Rowan Williams.

SIOS   The refrain to a song employing Psalm 139, com-
            posed by the monks of Weston Priory.

SK   *Songs of Kabir,* Kabir.

SL   *The Spiritual Life: Great Spiritual Truths for Everyday
            Life,* Evelyn Underhill.

SMF   *Seek My Face: A Jewish Mystical Theology,*
            Arthur Green.

SR   *Solitude and Resurrection,* Thomas Merton. CD.

SROGB   *Sutra of the Realization of Great Being,*
            Thich Nhat Hanh.

SSMT   *Seventh Step of Mindfulness Training,*
            Thich Nhat Hanh.

SWYA   *Start Where You Are: A Guide to Compassionate
            Living,* Pema Chodron.

TBLD   *The Tibetan Book of Living and Dying,*
            Sogal Rinpoche.

TBOA	*Three Books of Autolycus,* Theophilus of Antioch.
TCW	*The Catholic Worker,* "On Pilgrimage," September 1974, by Dorothy Day.
TH	*Transformation and Healing,* Thich Nhat Hanh. (The name he gave to his translation and commentary of the *Satipatthana Sutra,* the Sutra of the Four Establishments of Mindfulness.)
THGL	*The Hidden Ground of Love: Letters on Religious Experience and Social Concerns,* Thomas Merton, edited by William H. Shannon.
TI	*The Idiot,* Fyodor Dostoyevsky.
TIC	*The Interior Castle,* Theresa of Avila.
TIE	*The Inner Experience: Notes on Contemplation,* Thomas Merton.
TIM	*Trust in Mind (Hsin Shin Ming),* Tseng Ts'an. (Translated by Stanley Lombardo.)
TKAWAK	*To Know as We Are Known,* Parker Palmer.
TMLL	*Thomas Merton: A Life in Letters,* edited by William H. Shannon and Christine M. Bochen.
TP	*The Praktikos,* Evagrius of Pontis.
U	*Unpublished,* paraphrased by Sheila Trieff from Thich Nhat Hanh, http://dailymeditate.com.
U1	*Unpublished,* paraphrased by Rebecca Taylor from *Always We Begin Again: The Benedictine Way of Living,* John McQuiston II.
ULB	*The Unbearable Lightness of Being: God, Evolution, and the Power of Love,* Ilia Delio.
WAISI	*The World As I See It,* Albert Einstein.
WCT	*The Way of Chuang Tzu,* Thomas Merton.
WDDLRB	*Wisdom Distilled from Daily Living the Rule of Benedict,* Joan Chittister, OSB.
WIS	*Word into Silence,* John Mair, OSB.

WMUC   *What Makes Us Catholic: Eight Gifts for Life*, Thomas H. Groome, citing Patrick Kavanagh and Elizabeth Barrett Browning.

WNEPLK   *The Wisdom of No Escape and the Path of Loving Kindness*, Pema Chodron.

WOH   *With One Heart*, DVD of the 50th anniversary of Weston (Benedictine) Priory in Weston, Vermont.

YWTM   *A Year with Thomas Merton*, selected and edited by Jonathan Montaldo.

ZMBM   *Zen Mind, Beginner's Mind*, Shunryu Suzuki.

ZSCS   *Zen Spirit, Christian Spirit*, Robert Kennedy, SJ.

Contemplation (Meditation) Sessions

Author's note: Session 1 is longer than most sessions; it assumes a communal setting, people sitting together, and entails a little explanation of practice. I think twenty-five to thirty minutes is ordinarily an ideal time for communal practice. Intervals between spoken elements of guided meditations are suggested here. Suggested times assume time to speak *gatha* (prayer-poems, sayings, excerpts) between intervals of silence. Individual practice time is up to individuals.

Session 1

Contemplation (meditation) is returning to ourselves in the present moment through mindful breathing, through conscious breathing. This is gentle, deep, calm, grateful, peaceful breathing that enables inner stillness. We stop, we calm, we rest, we heal.

Ordinarily, we wear ourselves out with chatter. The chatter of our fears, reflections, regrets, anxieties, our worries and resentments, our anger, pain, and chaos, chatter of our desires and curiosities, of our projected plans and unfinished work (**WOH**)—with restlessness, discouragement, complaining, with the confused, chaotic, and self-seeking activity of the false self (**CP**). Chatter arises because we are "talking" (silently, inside ourselves) about <u>past</u> events and future possibilities (See Session 3, the *gatha* from *Zen Spirit, Christian Spirit* (**ZSCS**).

We practice mindful breathing, sitting like a mountain (**BL**), our belly up to the sky on the inhale and down into the earth on the exhale.

Everything in a guided mediation is designed to bring us back to the present moment in which we are one with our breathing:

- Bell
- Counting one's breath
- A lighted candle in the midst of the circle of practitioners
- Music
- A word or words (mantra)
- A *gatha*, a prayer-poem or saying (e.g., "Breathing in I see myself as a flower, breathing out I feel fresh. Flower . . . fresh!"). (**BL**)
- Visualizations
  Etc.

Always begin practice by stretching. Once seated invite your facial muscles to relax, then your neck and shoulders, down to your toes. But don't *try hard*, don't employ "arduous effort." Don't worry about distractions: "Do not try to stop your thinking. Let it stop by itself. If something comes into your mind let it come in, and let it go out. It will not stay long" (**ZMBM**). Contemplative (meditative) practice is the skill set achieved by not trying too hard: "You cannot find Buddha or Christ nature by arduous effort. Reality cannot be caught by the thinking, feeling mind. Moment after moment to watch your breathing, to watch your posture, is true nature. There is no secret beyond this point . . . How to sit is how to act" (**ZMBM**).

The practice I coach usually begins with me saying, "Brothers and Sisters (and, alternately, Sisters and Brothers), I wish you good meditation," while placing hands together, palms in alignment, raising them to the forehead, and bowing to other persons in the circle of practitioners. Practice ends with the same gesture, a bow and the words, again me speaking, "Sisters and Brothers (and, alternately, Brothers and Sisters), thank you for meditating with one another and with me." This beginning is hereafter referred to as *Commence*. And this conclusion is hereafter referred to as *Conclude*. (The commencing and concluding formulas will appear at the beginning and end of Session 1 and at the end of the book.)

Sisters and Brothers, I wish you good meditation.

> [Hereafter, "**Commence**" means to welcome sisters and brothers to meditate and to thank them for their practice.]

Invite the bell to intone, three times, with about fifteen seconds between each ring, or until the resonant sound of the bell has ceased.

Then,

"Breathing in I see myself as a flower
Breathing out I feel fresh."
1 bell

Breathing in I see myself as a mountain
Breathing out I feel solid.
1 bell

Breathing in I see myself as still water
Breathing out I reflect things as they are.
1 bell

Breathing in I see myself as space [empty space within and without]. Breathing out I feel free." (**BL**)

Interval: 1 minute

Flower . . . fresh.
Mountain . . . solid.
Still water . . . reflecting.
Space . . . free!

Interval: 2 minutes

"Keep you back straight, neck and head aligned with the spinal column, straight but not tight or wood-like. Now begin to follow your breath and to relax all of your muscles. As for everything else, let it go. Let go of everything. If you want to relax the worry-tightened muscles in your face, let a half-smile come to your face. As the half-smile appears, all the facial muscles begin to relax. Often it helps to meditate on the image of a pebble thrown into a river. Breathe slowly and deeply following each breath, becoming one with the breath. Then let go of everything. Imagine yourself as a pebble which has been thrown into a river. The pebble sinks through the water effortlessly. Detached from everything, it falls by the shortest distance possible, finally reaching the bottom, the point of perfect rest. You are like a pebble which has let itself fall into the river, letting go of everything. At the center of your being is your breath." (**MM**)

Interval: 2 minutes.

"Hold your being secure and quiet, keep your life collected in its own center. Do not allow your thoughts to be disturbed." (*WCT*)

Interval: 1 minute

"Breathe, you are alive." (*BYAA*)
1 bell

Brothers and Sisters, thank you for meditating with one another and with me.

(Hereafter, "**Conclude**" means thanking brothers and sisters for meditating with one another and with you.)

Session 2

Commence

3 bells

"Breathing in I calm my body
Breathing out I smile.
Dwelling in the present moment
I know this is a wonderful moment.

Interval: 1 minute

Breathing in I calm my feelings
Breathing out I smile.
Dwelling in the present moment
I know this is a wonderful moment.

Interval: 1 minute

Breathing in I calm the objects of the mind in me
Breathing out I smile.
Dwelling in the present moment
I know this is wonderful moment.

Interval: 1 minute

Breathing in I calm my mind—my whole self—
Breathing out I smile.
Dwelling in the present moment
I know this is a wonderful moment." (*BL*)
1 bell

Interval: 5 minutes

"Your breath should be light, even and flowing, like a thin stream of water flowing through the sand. Your breathing can flow gracefully like a river, like a water snake crossing the water and not like a chain of rugged mountains or the gallop of a horse. To master our breath is to be in control of our bodies and minds. Each time we find ourselves dispersed and find it difficult to gain control of ourselves the method of watching the breath can be used." (*MM*)

Interval: 5 minutes

"It is very helpful to realize that being here, sitting in meditation, doing simple everyday things like working, walking outside, talking with people, bathing, using the toilet, and eating, is actually all that we need to be fully wake, fully alive, fully human. Being satisfied with what we already have is a magical golden key to being alive in a full, unrestricted, and inspired way. One of the major obstacles to enlightenment is resentment, feeling cheated, holding a grudge about who you are, where you are, what you are. For some reason we don't feel satisfaction in a full and complete way. Meditation is a process of lightening up, of trusting the basic goodness of what we have and who we are, and of realizing that any wisdom that exists, exists in what we already have." (*WNEPLK*)

Interval: 2 minutes

"If you practice mindful breathing, mindful walking, you become free of your past, free of your future, free of your projects." (*AWFCF*).
1 bell

Conclude

Session 3

Commence

1 bell

"Breathe and be one with the air that you breathe.
Breathe and be one with the river that flows
Breathe and be one with the earth that you tread.
Breathe and be one with the fire that glows.
Breathe and you break the thought of birth and death.
Breathe and you see that impermanence is life." (***BYAA***)
1 bell

We return to ourselves in the present moment, through mindful breathing, through conscious breathing, perhaps inhaling to the silent count of "one," deep, gentle inhalation, and breathing out to the count of one, a full exhale. Two on the inhale, two on the exhale up to the number we choose.
1 bell

In this fashion we are "fully awake, fully active, fully aware that we are alive." (***CP***)
And we touch our inner core of goodness,
our inner core of peaceful stillness,
our inner core of freedom.
1 bell

Interval: 5 minutes

Remember: "Breathing in I see myself as space [empty space], breathing out I feel free." "Emptiness is the ground of everything. Thanks to emptiness, everything is possible. Emptiness is an optimistic concept. If I am not empty I cannot be here. And if you are not empty, you cannot be there. If we are not empty we become a block of matter. To be empty means to be alive, to breathe in and breathe out. We cannot be alive if we are not empty." (*BP*)

Interval: 5 minutes

"Call it Being, call it *Atman*, call it *Pneuma*, or Silence" (*TMLL*) or call it the Divine, the Holy One, or the Holy, or God.

"'My name is I am.' The Holy paused.
I waited. The Holy continued,
'When you live in the past,
With its mistakes and regrets,
It is hard. I'm not there.
My name is not I was. When
you live in the future,
With its problems and fears,
It is hard. I am not there.
My name is not I will be.

"When you live in this moment,
It is not hard. I am here.
My name is I am." (*ZSCS*)

Interval: 5 minutes

"Life is filled with suffering, but it is also filled with many wonders, like the blue sky, the sunshine, the face of a baby. To suffer is not enough. If we are peaceful, if we are happy, we can smile and blossom like a flower, and everyone in our family, our entire society will benefit from our peace. Do we need to make a special effort to enjoy the beauty of the blue sky? Do we have to practice to enjoy it? No, we just enjoy it." (*BP*)

Interval: 5 minutes

"Mindful breathing, mindful walking; train yourself to drink tea mindfully, to become a free person while drinking tea. Train yourself to become a free person while making breakfast." (*AWFCF*)
3 bells

Conclude

Session 4

Note to the reader: This is the first of several practice sessions in which the elements of "guidedness" are taken almost entirely from one source. The source from which the elements of guidedness in this session are taken is *Meister Eckhart's Book of the Heart: Meditations for the Restless Soul* (**MEBH**). In this book Jon M. Sweeney and Mark S. Burrows engage in something remarkably parallel to what Thomas Merton did in his *The Way of Chuang Tsu*. In their words, "The poems found here are not a translation, but rather our attempts at voicing—or re-voicing—his thought." As with Merton's re-voicing of Chuang Tsu, Sweeney and Burrows capture the voice of a thirteenth-century mystic, whom they describe as "the Christian Rumi, the ecstatic Catholic's Kabir, the Dominican Hafiz," with remarkable faithfulness.

Commence

1 bell

"The Bell of Mindfulness is the voice of the [Holy One] calling us back to ourselves. We should respect this sound, stop thinking and talking, and return to ourselves with breathing and a smile." (**BYAA**)
1 bell
Interval: 3 minutes

"My life is like a page on which
So much is written:

Hurts and [sorrows] and the tumble
Of fears and uncertainties.

What You want of me, God, is
That I clean the slate, emptying

It of all this to make room for
The freedom of nothingness

Where alone You, my God
Have room to grow.
1 bell
Interval: 5 minutes

In my hurry I often
Forget that You desire

to seek those who
have gone astray,
even me, and that
my work is to free
myself of myself
so that you can be

born in me, and so
your joy in seeking

meets my joy in
having been found.

Interval: 5 minutes

"How should I prepare to find You?
in emptying myself of the chatter

of my words, and opening myself
to the silence that allows me

to risk an unknowing that expects
nothing and deserves nothing

and wills nothing other than
the word You speak in

the stillness I keep where
my wandering ceases

and my wondering begins.

Interval: 5 minutes

"In distress and want I ask 'Where, O God, are you?'
Here, I am as close to you as the warmth of your breath.

But this does not satisfy my mind, so I ask again.
Here, in the confusions that make you trade life for death.

Still, I ask [what I have already asked].
Here, in the doubts that rise against my descending truths.

And yet I am undone with deceptions ever old and new.
Here, let me give Myself to you with love that alone will sooth.

Interval: 5 minutes

"I want more love
Which is to say
More God.
I want more God
in everything

More love.

In everything.

In and through and
beyond it all

More God."
1 bell

Conclude

Session 5

Commence

"Moment after moment, to watch our breathing, is true nature."
(**ZMBM**)
1 bell

"Moment after moment, to watch our posture
is true nature."(**ZMBM**)
1 bell

"Moment after moment, to watch our breathing, to watch our posture is true nature. There is no secret beyond this point. How to sit is how to act." (**ZMBM**)
1 bell
Interval: 5 minutes

"The fall in the book of Genesis is our fall into this present mode of consciousness, where everything is divided, centered on itself, and set in conflict with others. The fall is the fall into self-consciousness, into a consciousness centered in the self which has lost touch with the eternal ground of consciousness, which is the true Self." (**PHC**)[1]

Interval: 5 minutes

"For Diadochos the origin of evil is not explained by a struggle between the powers of light and darkness but by the power of human imagination. 'When in the desire of their heart someone conceives and gives form to what in reality has no existence, then what they desire begins to exist.'" (**PHC**)

---

1. Quoting Bede Griffith.

Interval: 5 minutes

"Master Tung-Kuo asked Chuang Tzu, 'This thing called *Tao*—where does it exist?' Chuang Tzu said, 'There's no place it doesn't exist.' 'Come,' said Master Tung Kuo, 'you must be more specific.' 'It is in the ant.' 'As low a thing as that?' 'It is in the simple grass.' 'But that's lower still!' 'It is in the tiles and shards.' 'How can it be so low?' 'It is in the dung.' Master Tung Kuo made no reply." (***PHC***)

Interval: 5 minutes

"Religious people are no doubt aware that God is in them and not merely that God comes to them, and that the very center of their soul is God's dwelling place. They likewise know that God is in all things; and in order to meet God they plunge deep within themselves and within all things, in pursuit of their own and God's final secret. The more they do this the more they discover the truth of God's presence, even more luminous, more elemental. They then search in the depths of their hearts for a place where they might as it were stand and contemplate this Presence, the inner sanctum where their own incommunicable individuality issues from Being itself and springs into existence." (***SCAAE***)

Interval: 3 minutes

"Taste and see that the Holy One is good. Happy are those who take refuge in God" (Ps 34).
1 bell

Conclude

Session 6

Commence

1 bell

"When we practice *zazen*, seated meditation, our mind always follows our breathing." (**ZMBM**)
1 bell

"Do not be bothered by anything. *Zen* is not some kind of excitement, but concentration on our usual everyday routine. If you become too busy and too excited, your mind becomes rough and ragged. But if your mind is calm and constant, you can keep yourself away from the noisy world even though you are in the midst of it. In the midst of noise and change, your mind will be quiet and stable." (**ZMBM**)
1 bell

Interval: 5 minutes

"A wave on the ocean has a beginning and an end, a birth and a death. But the wave is empty. The wave is full of water, but it is empty of a separate self. A wave is a form which has been made possible thanks to the existence of wind and water. If a wave only sees its form, with its beginning and end, it will be afraid of birth and death. But if the wave sees that it is water, then it will be emancipated from birth and death. Each wave is born and is going to die. But the water is free from birth and death." (**HOU**)

Interval: 5 minutes

"Most of us live much of our lives caught in the whirlwind of the stories going on in our heads. As our contemplative practice matures, we are presented with opportunities to drop the story and look straight into these thoughts and feelings which lead us around by a nose ring. And we see they are without substance. Without the story they have no power. This insight is behind Mark Twain's famous line, 'I'm an old man now and have had a great many problems. Most of them never happened.' A lot goes on in our heads that is quite worthless. The silent self knows that what sees the fear, the pain, the inner chaos, is free of the fear, pain, or chaos. But for the noisy mind it all becomes a huge problem." (*ISL*)

Interval: 5 minutes

If we are religious, "Zen reminds us that the highest point of our mysticism is reached not in the experience that I know God or that I love God but in the experience that God lives in us." If we are Christian, "Zen reminds us that contemplation is not looking at Christ, or a following of Christ, but a transformation into Christ." (*ZSCS*)
1 bell
Interval: 7 minutes

"Live Christ!" (*ISL*)
1 bell

Conclude

Session 7

Note to the reader: All the elements of this guided meditation are taken from one source: *Songs of Kabir,* translated by Rabindranath Tagore, assisted by Evelyn Underhill.

Commence

3 bells

"O servant where do you seek me? Lo! I am beside you.
I am neither in temple nor in mosque:
    I am neither in Kaaba nor in
    Kailash:
Neither am I in rites and ceremonies,
    Nor in Yoga and renunciation.
If you are a true seeker, you shall at
    once see Me: you shall meet Me
    In a moment of time.
Kabir says, 'O Sadhu! The Divine is the
    Breath of all breath.'"

Interval: 7 minutes

"Bathe in the truth, know the true Guru,
Have faith in the true Name!
Kabir says 'It is the Spirit of the
quest which helps; I am the slave
of this Spirit of the quest.' All
things are created by *OM;*
The love form is *OM's,* is love's
body. *OM* is without form,
without
Quality, without decay.

Seek union with *OM*."
1 bell

Interval: 7 minutes

All things are created by *OM*;
The love-form is *OM's* body.
OM is without form, without quality
Without decay;
Seek union with *OM*.
But the Formless One takes a thousand
forms in the eyes of the creatures: Pure
and indestructible,
Infinite and fathomless,
When the Formless One dances in rapture, waves of
form arise from the dance.
The body and the mind cannot contain
themselves, when they are touched by
the Formless One's great joy.
The Formless One is immersed in all consciousness, all
joys, and all sorrows;
The Formless One has no beginning and no end
And holds everything in bliss.
1 bell

Interval: 7 minutes

3 bells

Conclude

Session 8

Commence

3 bells

"Breath returns to God who gave it" (Eccl 12:7).
1 bell
Interval: 1 minute

"To pray is to gain a sense of the mystery that animates all beings, the divine margins in all attainments. Prayer is our humble answer to the inconceivable surprise of living. It is all we can offer in return for the mystery by which we live." (*IAFW*)
1 bell
Interval: 5 minutes

"Who is worthy to be present at the constant unfolding of time? Amidst the meditation of mountains, the humility of flowers—wiser than all alphabets—clouds that die constantly for the sake of God's glory, we are hating, hunting, and hurting. Suddenly we feel ashamed of our clashes and complaints in the face of the tacit glory in nature." (*IAFW*)
1 bell
Interval: 5 minutes

"It is so embarrassing to live! How strange we are in the world, and how presumptuous our doings! Only one response can maintain us: gratefulness for witnessing the wonder, for the gift of our unearned right to serve, to adore, and to fulfill. It is gratefulness that makes the soul great!" (*IAFW*)
Interval: 5 minutes

"Up to now I only heard of you by the hearing of my ear. But now I see you with the eyes of my heart. Therefore, although I am still suffering, I will stop living in dust and ashes and I will not be sorrowful" (Job 42:5f).[1]

Interval: 5 minutes

"Your steadfast love O God never ceases, your mercies never come to an end. They are new everyone morning so great is your faithfulness" (Lam 3:22).[2]
3 bells

Conclude

1. This is an interpretation by Gustavo Gutierrez of the end (chapter 42) of the book of Job. (*OJGTSI*). And, "eyes of the heart" is from Saint Augustine. (*CSA*)

2. This translation of Lamentations 3:22 is indebted to the Benedictine monks off Weston Priory, Weston, VT.

Session 9

Note to the reader: All elements of this guided meditation are taken from one source: Dom Henri Le Saux, OSB, writing as Swami Abhishiktananda (after journeying to India and living Christianity in a Hindu context). The excerpts used to guide practice are all taken from his book, *Saccidananda: A Christian Approach to Advaitic Experience,* a text that makes frequent reference to a Hindu teacher, Sri Ramana Maharshi, who was influential for Dom Le Saux. (*SCAAE*)

Commence

3 bells

"There was one breathing exercise Sri Ramana recommended. This was to fix attention on the act of breathing and consciously to follow the process of inhaling and exhaling."
1 bell
Interval: 1 minute

"Such attention and concentration on inhaling and exhaling of itself establishes a rhythm and automatically slows down the rate of breathing."
1 bell
Interval: 12 minutes

"The movement of the mind soon adjusts itself correspondingly, becomes more regular, slows down in its turn and makes room for inner silence."
1 bell
Interval: 5 minutes

"To any who sought him out and sincerely asked what to do to progress spiritually, Sri Ramana regularly recommended the practice of asking the mental question, Who am I? That is to say, the quest for and pursuit of the Self within the self, beyond all external manifestations, piercing through to the deepest centers of consciousness in trying to find out in every instant, in every act, who in truth it is that lives, thinks and acts, being attentive to the see-er in the act of seeing, the hearer in the act of hearing. Constantly, relentlessly, pursuing this consciousness of oneself which hides behind the appearances and events of one's psychic life, of discovering it, seizing it in its original purity before anything else has covered it over or adulterated it."

Interval: 5 minutes

"Thus seized, consciousness of oneself has to be held in the fine point of the spirit to prevent it from escaping again. This means trying to reach oneself, one's identity, beyond and beneath the level of manifestation, the superficial level. Sri Ramana was perfectly sure that this persistent but calm proceeding could not fail to bear fruit. The phenomenal self, the surface-I, if pursued to its last stronghold, will in the end disappear as if by magic, like a thief surprised in the act who runs for dear life. The essential I will then shine in solitary glory in a consciousness which has been stilled, and will fill it entirely."

Interval: 5 minutes

"Follow the process of inhaling and exhaling. Ask who is the I who lives, thinks, acts, sees, hears. Pursue the consciousness of oneself that hides behind appearances. Make the surface-I disappear. Then the essential-I will shine in solitary glory, stilled."

Interval: 5 minutes

"Down to the place whence springs the I, plunge within thyself like the diver searching for the pearl." (*BG*)

1 bell

Conclude

Session 10

3 bells

"Meditation is the very simple process by which we prepare ourselves, in the first instance, to be at peace with ourselves so that we are capable of appreciating the peace of the Godhead within us. The longer we meditate the more we become aware that the source of our newfound calm in our daily lives is precisely the life of God within us." (**WIS**)

Breathe God. *1 bell*
Interval: 1 minute

"The degree of peace we possess is directly proportional to our awareness of this fact of life, [that the Godhead is within us], a fact of human consciousness, common to every man and every woman in the world. But to realize this fact as a present reality in our lives, we have to decide that we want to be at peace. This is the reason for the psalmist's saying 'Be still and know that I am God'" (Ps 46:10). (**WIS**)
Breathe God.
1 bell
Interval: 1 minute

"Meditation simplifies us, simplifies us to the point where we can receive the fullness of truth and the fullness of love. It prepares us and enables us to listen with childlike attention to the Spirit within us. As we persevere in meditation, we enter ever more deeply into relationship with this Spirit, with God who is love dwelling in our hearts." (**WIS**)

Breathe God.

Interval: 7 minutes

Saint Athanasius wrote of Antony: "His soul being free of confusion, he held his outer senses undisturbed, so that from the soul's joy his face was cheerful. He was never troubled, his soul being calm, and he never looked gloomy, his mind being joyous. For the desert monastics true life began when one was no longer a prisoner of such feelings as anger, fear, lust, and pride." (**SGH**)

Interval: 5 minutes

"A happiness that is sought for ourselves alone can never be found: for happiness that is diminished by being shared is not big enough to make us happy. There is a false and momentary happiness in self-satisfaction, but it always leads to sorrow because it narrows and deadens our spirit. True happiness is found in unselfish love, a love that increases in proportion as it is shared." (**MPN**)

Interval: 5 minutes

"The inner self is precisely that self which cannot be tricked or manipulated by anyone. The true self is like a very shy wild animal that never appears at all whenever an alien presence is at hand, and comes out only when all is peaceful, in silence, when the true self is untroubled and alone. The true self cannot be lured by anyone or anything because the true self responds to no lure except that of the divine freedom." (**TIE**)

Interval: 5 minutes

"God and your true self are not separate." (**FCP**) "God is your being, and what you are you are in God." (**CU**)
1 bell

Conclude

Session 11

Commence

3 bells

"Do not lose yourself in dispersion and in your surroundings. Practice mindful breathing to return to what is happening in the present moment." (*FMT*)
1 bell
Interval: 1 minute

"Be in touch with what is wondrous, refreshing, and healing in yourself and around you" (*FMT*)
1 bell
Interval: 1 minute

"Plant seeds of peace, joy and understanding in yourself in order to facilitate the work of transformation in the depths of your consciousness." (*FMT*)

Interval: 5 minutes

"Prayer," commencing always in "the setting aside of thought" (*TP*) "never touches us as long as it remains on the surface of our lives, as long as it is nothing but one more of a thousand things that must be done. It is only when prayer becomes 'the one thing necessary' that real prayer begins. Prayer begins to take on its full dimensions only when we begin to intuit that the subtle nothingness of prayer is everything. Prayer begins when we go to our place of prayer as to a sacred place, when we realize that our own heart is the place where Jacob's ladder touches the earth." (*MPN*)

Interval: 5 minutes

"In prayer we sit and we are lost before we begin. Prayer appears before us as a kind of palace with no doors. The palace is nowhere and the path leading to it has no sign saying 'enter here.' We find ourselves in a solitary silence that skirts the edge of the abyss that is at once our own nothingness and the plenitude of God. In prayer, if we follow it through enough, we eventually come face to face with the fundamental question of life—How can we find the One who fills all things yet escapes our grasp? How can we find our way to God?" (*MPN*)

Interval: 5 minutes

"God is all about us and within us, dancing away as the primordial rhythms of our breathing, as each new day gives way to the night which gives way to emergence of a new day. God is dancing away inviting us. As Merton has said," (*MPN*) "We are invited to forget ourselves on purpose, cast our awful solemnity to the wind, and join in the general Dance." (*NMI*) "Then, we unexpectedly awaken to our true self, one with God, in the midst of our fragility and our wayward ways." (*MPN*)

Interval: 5 minutes

"When we practice mindful breathing, mindful walking, we become free of our past, free of our future, free of our projects and we are available to ourselves in the present moment." (*AWFCF*)
3 bells

Conclude

29

Session 12

Commence

1 bell

Stop
Breathe
Be still
1 bell
Interval: 1 minute

Pay attention
Look deeply
Be present
1 bell
Interval: 1 minute

Let go
Be empty
Free!

Still, present, free.

Interval: 5 minutes

"We do not live merely in order to 'do something'—no matter what. On the contrary, some of us need to discover that we will not begin to live more fully until we have the courage to do and see and taste and experience much less than usual. Our being is not enriched merely by activity or experience as such. A multitude of badly performed actions and of experiences only half-lived exhaust and deplete our being. By doing things badly we make ourselves less real." (***NMI***)

Interval: 3 minutes

"What is meant by a true woman, a true man? The true women and men of old were not afraid. If they failed no sorrow. No self-congratulations in success." (**WCT**)

Interval: 1 minute

"The true men and women of old slept without dreams and woke without worries. They breathed from their heels not from their bellies. They knew no dread of death. Their entrance was without gladness. Their exit without resistance." (**WCT**)
1 bell
Interval: 2 minute

"Minds free, thoughts gone, brows clear, faces serene. Were they cool? Only cool as autumn. Were they hot? Not hotter than spring. All that came out of them came quiet, like the four seasons." (**WCT**)

Interval: 5 minutes
"God knows the time and place to deliver you and therefore you must resign yourself wholly to God. It is God's concern to help, and to deliver from all confusion." (**IC**) What God delivers from is confusion.

Interval: 5 minutes

"Let everything go. Feelings change like the clouds. Your breath is your anchor." (**U**)

Interval: 3 minutes

"Your breath is your anchor."

3 bells

Conclude

Session 13

Note to the reader: With the exception of the opening *gatha* on breathing, and a portion repeated at the conclusion of practice, the content of this meditation is derived entirely from *The Rule of Benedict*, **RB**, chapter seven on humility, paraphrased and shortened.

Commence

3 bell

"Breathe and you know that you are alive.
Breathe and you know that all is helping you.
Breathe and you know that you are the world
Breathe and you know that the flower is breathing too.
Breathe for yourself and you breathe for the world.
Breathe in compassion and breathe out joy."(***BYAA***)

1 bell

Interval: 5 minutes

The Rule of Benedict, Prologue: "Listen carefully my sons and daughters to these instructions, attend to them with the ear of your heart. This is advice from a father/mother who loves you; welcome it and faithfully put it into practice."

Chapter Seven: the twelve steps of humility:

1. Keep wonder and awe for God and God's creation ever before you.

2. Do not think of yourself and your desires as the center of all things.

3. Listen to others, especially the wise.

Interval: 5 minutes

4. When you experience setbacks and suffering do not fall into self-centeredness, but train your heart to embrace the life you have.

5. Seek wise counsel in all things doubtful.

6. Live simply.

Interval: 5 minutes

7. Do not cultivate an overblown sense of importance, but nurture modesty in yourself.

8. Listen to people who have thoughtfully assessed their experiences.

9. Do not speak too much; cultivate silence.

Interval: 5 minutes

10. Do not laugh at what is not funny.

11. Let your speech be gentle, serious, modest, brief, and reasonable.

12. Let the way you hold yourself bespeak that you do not judge yourself the center of everything.

Interval: 5 minutes

"Breathe in compassion and breathe out joy."

1 bell

Conclude

Session 14

Commence

1 bell

"Let the remembrance of Jesus be with your every breath. Then indeed you will appreciate the value of stillness." (**LDA**)

"With your breathing combine watchfulness and the name of Jesus." (**OW-P**)
1 bell

"Having collected your mind, lead it into the channel of breathing through which air reaches the heart and, together with this inhaled air, allow your mind to descend into the heart and to remain there." (**AMPD**)
1 bell
Interval: 5 minutes

"Behold my beloved, I have shown you the power of silence, how thoroughly it heals and how fully pleasing it is to God. Wherefore I have written to you to show yourselves strong in this work you have undertaken, so that you may know that it was by silence that the saints grew, it was because of silence that the power of God dwelt in them, because of silence that the mysteries of God were made known to them." (Ammonas, cited in **CP**)

Interval: 5 minutes

"Silence teaches us God is not absent from us, but we are absent from God. If we can learn this lesson from the discipline of silence, we will be led into the discipline of solitude where the evasive self can be transformed by truth and love." (**TKAWAK**)

34

Interval: 5 minutes

"However quietly we speak, the Holy One is so near that the Holy One will hear us. We need no wings to go in search of God but have only to find a place where we can be alone and look upon the Holy One present within us."(*TIC*)

Interval: 5 minutes

"God is 'The Silent Infinite.'" (*EWS*)
1 bell

Conclude

Session 15

Commence

3 bells
Interval: 3 minutes

"Breathe for your joy to be steady and calm.
Breathe for your sorrow to flow away.
Breathe to renew every cell in your blood.
Breathe to renew the depths of consciousness.
Breathe and you dwell in the here and now.
Breathe and all you touch is new and real." (***BYAA***)

Interval: 5 minutes

"We are deprived through words of an authentic intimacy with what we are or what the Other is. We need poetry not to regain this intimacy, which is impossible, but to remember we miss it and to prove to ourselves the value of those moments when we are able to encounter other people, or trees, or anything, beyond words, in silence." (***NYT***).[1]

Interval: 5 minutes

"Morally adult choices flow from the center of our receptivity to being, in resonance with fellow travelers on earth. Then our actions have a gentleness that lessens the violence in the world." (***NLS***) "Anything is or has being in proportion to the degree in which it is a subjectivity in possession of itself." (***C***)[2]

Interval: 5 minutes

1. Quoting Yves Bonnefoy.
2. Quoting Karl Rahner, SJ.

"We recall the past; we anticipate the future as if we found it too slow in coming. We are so unwise that we wander around in times that do not belong to us, and not think of the only one that does." (*P*)

Interval: 5 minutes

Then Moses asked God, "What, shall I tell Pharaoh, is the name of the God of the Israelites?" And God answered, "Tell Pharaoh, the name of the God who sends you is 'I am present with you'"(Exod 3:13f).[3]

1 bell

Conclude

---

3. A midrash identified by Everett Fox, *The Five Books of Moses.*

Session 16

Note to the reader: This is a meditation for Christmastime.

Commence

1 bell

"Faith in Jesus as the Christ implies we recognize in Jesus our own human-divine self, the self that bares God's image and is alive with God's own breath." (**DTW**)
1 bell

Alive with God's own breath.
1 bell

Alive with God's own breath.
1 bell
Interval: 5 minutes

We are given a child—vulnerable, in need, simple. We must be vulnerable and simple and acknowledge our need—so that the Holy One reigns in our hearts.

Interval: 5 minutes

Shepherds and kings are watchful. We must be watchful.

"Tell us shepherds, what have you seen? Who has appeared on earth? We have seen a newborn infant, and a choir of angels praising God, alleluia." (**CPB**)

Interval: 5 minutes

"Only one way to be a disciple—grow young again. This means learning how to die, to make oneself free, a traveler with almost no baggage, no acquired positions, no regrets, no decorations. Let the only dream of your life be—to wake up. Nothing is more revolutionary than childhood." (**ML**)

Interval: 5 minutes

"Let peace dwell in you so as to kindle others" (St. Augustine, Sermon 353.7).

Alive with God's own breath.
1 bell

Conclude

Session 17

Commence

1 bell

"Breathing in I calm my body
Breathing out I smile.

Breathing in I calm my feelings.
Breathing out I smile."
1 bell

"Breathing in I calm my whole self.
Breathing out I smile." (**BL**)
1 bell

Interval: 5 minutes

"In the morning light may I glimpse again the
divine image within me, the threads of eternal
glory woven into the fabric of every man and
woman. Again may I catch the sight of the mystery
of the human soul fashioned in the Divine likeness
deeper than knowing, more enduring than time.
And in glimpsing these threads of light amidst the
Weakness and distortions of my life
Let me be recalled to the strength and beauty
Deep in my soul. Let me be recalled to the strength
And beauty of the Divine image in every living
Soul." (**CB**)
1 bell

Interval: 6 minutes

"Glory be for the gift of life
Unfolding through those who have gone before us.
Glory be for Divine life planted within our souls.
Glory be for the grace of new beginnings
Placed before us in every moment and encounter of life.
Glory, glory, glory
for the grace of new beginnings in every moment of life."(*CB*)
1 bell

Interval: 6 minutes

"Dwelling in the present moment, I know this is a wonderful moment." (*BL*)
3 bells

Conclude

Session 18

Commence

1 bell

Return to yourself in the present moment through mindful breathing, through conscious breathing; (pause) gentle, deep, calm,
grateful, peaceful breathing.
1 bell

One on the inhale, one on the exhale (pause) two on the inhale,
two on the exhale, (pause) and so on counting one's breath.
1 bell

Your stomach goes up to the sky on the inhale, down into the earth
on the exhale.

Interval: 7 minutes

"Companions, the wise tell us that God abides in silence, that God
abides in the silence of our hearts. Let us not speak of silence,
rather let silence speak to us of God. Together, let us enter through
the door of serenity the silence of our hearts." (**WOH**)

Interval: 5 minutes

"The hearts of the wise are tranquil, mirrors of heaven and earth,
the glass of everything. Emptiness, stillness, tranquility, tasteless-
ness, silence, non-action: this is the level of heaven and earth. This
is perfect Tao. Wise women and men find here their resting place.
Resting, they are empty."(**WCT**)

Interval: 5 minutes

"Contemplation is the way out of the great self-centered psychodrama. When interior silence is discovered, compassion flows. If we deepen our inner silence, our compassion for others deepens. We cannot pass through the doorways of silence without becoming part of God's embrace of all humanity in its suffering and joy." (*ISL*)

Interval: 5 minutes

"In all creation there is nothing so like God as stillness." (*MEMT*)
1 bell

Conclude

Session 19

1 bell

Practice mindful breathing, conscious breathing, so that you notice what you are doing. "When the Buddha was asked, 'What do you monks practice?' he replied, 'We sit, we walk, and we eat.' The questioner continued 'But everyone sits, walks, and eats.' And the Buddha replied 'When we sit, we *know* we are sitting. When we walk, we *know* we are walking. When we eat, we *know* we are eating.'" (*LBLC*)

1 bell

"Mindful breathing, mindful walking: free of our past, free of our future, free of our projects" (*AWFCF*)

1 bell

"Do what you are doing." (*SE*)

1 bell

Interval: 7 minutes

"Surely one of the great gifts of Creation is found in the two daily periods of the change of light, the hours of dawn and dusk. Know this day. Being awake and aware as the sun rises and the sun sets can make a difference in our religious lives that cannot be over-estimated." (*SMF*)

Interval: 5 minutes

"Contemplation is the highest expression of [a person's] intellectual and spiritual life. It is that life itself, fully awake, fully active,

fully aware that [we] are alive. It is spiritual wonder. It is spontaneous awe at the sacredness of life, of being. It is gratitude for life,
for awareness and for being. It is vivid realization that life and
being in us proceed from an invisible, transcendent and infinitely
abundant source. Contemplation is, above all, awareness of the
reality of that Source." (**CP**)

Interval: 5 minutes

"We should be able to live each day deeply, with joy, peace, and
compassion. Each morning I offer a stick of incense to the Buddha.
I promise myself that I will enjoy every minute of the day that is
given to me to live. It is thanks to the practice of mindful walking
and mindful breathing that I can enjoy deeply every moment of
my daily life." (**AWFCF**)

Interval: 5 minutes

"Mindful breathing and mindful walking are like two friends, always helping me to delve into the here and the now and touch the
wonders of life that are available." (**AWFCF**)

Conclude

Session 20

Commence

1 bell

As soon as anger or hatred arise, turn your attention to your breath in order to see and understand the nature of your anger and hatred. (*FMT*)
1 bell

Turn your attention to your breath.
1 bell

Turn your attention to your breath.

Interval: 5 minutes

"When possessed by a sadness, an anxiety, a hatred, or passion, the method of pure observation and recognition may seem difficult. If so, turn to meditation on a fixed object, using your own state of mind as meditation's subject. We should treat our anxiety, our pain, our hatred, and passion gently, respectfully, not resisting it, but living with it, making peace with it, penetrating into its nature by meditation on interdependence." (*MM*)

Interval: 5 minutes

"You can make a mistake only when you forget that the other person suffers. The nectar of compassion is so wonderful. If you are committed to keeping it alive, then you are protected. What the other person says will not touch off the anger and irritation in you, because compassion is the real antidote for anger." (*AWFCF*)

Interval: 5 minutes

"Do not avoid contact with the suffering or close your eyes before suffering. Do not lose awareness of the existence of suffering in the life of the world. Find ways to be with those who are suffering including personal contact, images, and sound. Awaken yourself and others to the reality of suffering in the world." (**FMT**)

Interval: 5 minutes

"Moment by moment to watch your breath, to watch your postures, this is true nature."(**ZMBM**)

1 bell

Conclude

Session 21

Commence

1 bell

Breathe! "Train wholeheartedly."(*SWYA*)
Breathe! "Live wholeheartedly."
1 bell
Breathe! "Die wholeheartedly moment by moment."
1 bell

Interval: 5 minutes

"Of that which we dread, Healer God, make us fearless.
O Generous One, assist us with your help.
May the air we breath sweep fearlessness into us, fearlessness on earth,
fearlessness in heaven.
May fearlessness be our guard in front and behind us. May fearlessness encompass us above and below.
May we lose all fear of friend and enemy. May we not fear the known or the unknown. May we not fear the night or the day.
This day may all the world be our friend." (*IGP*)

Interval: 5 minutes

"The Way is calm and wide, not easy, not difficult.
But small minds get lost, hurrying, they fall behind.
Clinging, they go too far, sure to make a wrong turn. Just let it be!
In the end Nothing goes, nothing stays.

Follow nature and find the Way, free, easy, an undisturbed.
Tied to your thoughts you lose the truth, become, heavy, dull, and
unwell.

Not well, the mind is troubled.
So why hold or reject anything?" (**TIM**)

Interval: 5 minutes

"When you produce peace and happiness in yourself, you begin to
realize peace for the whole world. When you practice sitting mediation, if you enjoy even one moment of your sitting, you establish
serenity and happiness inside yourself, and you provide the world
a solid base for peace. If you do not begin your peace work with
yourself, where will you go to begin it? To sit, to smile, to look at
things and really see them, these are the basis of peace work." (**HU**)

Interval: 5 minutes

"If you are willing to feel fully and acknowledge your own sadness
and the sadness of life, but at the same time not be drowned by
it, because you also remember the vision and power of the Great
Eastern Sun[1]—that is, *the quality of being continually awake*—you
experience balance and completeness and you can hold them both
in your heart, which is actually the purpose of practice. As a result
of that, you can make a proper cup of tea." (**WNEPLK**)

Interval: 3 minutes

1. The term is from the Tibetan Buddhist way. It is remarkably like Gerard
Manley Hopkins's reference to the "Holy Ghost" coming from the east in his
poem "God's Grandeur."

Train wholeheartedly, Live wholeheartedly. Die to anxiety and resentment wholeheartedly. Breath wholeheartedly! (*SWYA*)
3 bells

Conclude

Session 22

Commence

"Moment after moment, to watch your breathing, to watch your posture, this is true nature." (**ZMBM**).
1 bell

"to watch your breathing, to watch your posture." (**ZMBM**)
1 bell

"to watch your breathing." (**ZMBM**)

Interval: 5 minutes

"The human mind is always searching for possessions and never feels fulfilled. This causes impure actions ever to increase. The wise always remember the principle of having few desires. *Bodhisattvas* live a simple life in peace in order to practice the Way, and consider the realization of perfect understanding as their only career." (**SROGB**)

Interval: 5 minutes

"Fidelity to grace in my life is fidelity to simplicity, rejecting analysis and ambition and elaborate thought and even elaborate concern." (**AYWTM**) Purity of heart: "childlike simplicity, clarity of purpose, and fine moral discrimination." (**PHC**) Every day I am a day old; the child who is God." (**OMWH**—Thomas Merton)

Interval: 5 minutes

We are built for contemplation. Communion with God in the silence of the heart is a God-given capacity like the rhododendron's capacity to flower, the fledgling's for flight, and the child's for self-forgetful abandon and joy." (*ISL*)

Interval: 5 minutes

"Moment after moment to watch your breathing, to watch your posture, this is true nature." (*ZMBM*)
3 bells

Conclude

Session 23

Commence

1 bell

"Persevering, fully awake, beyond all attachment and aversion, with steadfast meditative stability, the practitioner will attain the First Factor of Awakening, full attention." (***BYAA***)

"Beyond all attachment and aversion." (***BYAA***)

1 bell

"Steadfast meditative stability." (***BYAA***)

1 bell

Interval: 5 minutes

"Each day brings new failures. I become impatient; I worry about small things and take other people for granted; I give in to distractions and remain inattentive to signs of grace; I daydream about heroic deeds, while neglecting countless opportunities for charity." (***SGH***)

Interval: 5 minutes

"Look around you at the gifts of God, the clear sky, the pure air, the tender grass, the birds; nature is beautiful and sinless, and we, only we, are sinful and foolish, and we don't understand that life is heaven, for we have only to understand that and it will at once be fulfilled in all its beauty, we shall embrace one another and weep." (Father Zossima in *Brothers Karamazov*, quoted in ***SGH***)

Interval: 5 minutes

"Contemplative prayer is the world in which God can do any-thing. To move into that realm is the greatest adventure. It is to be open to the infinite and hence to infinite possibilities. Our private self-made worlds come to an end; a new world appears in us and around us and the impossible becomes an everyday experience." (*FCP*)

Interval: 5 minutes

"Steadfast meditative stability." (*BYAA*)

Conclude

Session 24

3 bells

"Mindful breathing, mindful walking." (***AWFCF***) Mindful sitting.

(Sustained pause)

3 bells

"We walk all the time, but usually it is more like running. When we walk like that, we print anxiety and sorrow on the earth." (***BP***)

Interval: 5 minutes

"Our mind can be tied up by sorrows and memories of the past; or drawn along by anxieties and predictions concerning the future or held subservient to feelings of irritation, fear, and doubt in the present; or obscured and confused by inaccurate perceptions." (***BYAA***)

Interval: 5 minutes

"We have to walk in a way that we only print peace and serenity on the Earth. Everyone of us can do that provided that we want it very much. Any child can do that. If we can take one step like that, we can take two, three, four, five. When we are able to take one step peacefully, happily, we are for the cause of peace and happiness for the whole of humankind." (***BP***)

Interval: 5 minutes

"It is the same as when we try to take knots out of thread. We have to be calm, and we need to take time. By observing our mind in all its subtlety, in a calm and self-contained way, we can free our mind from all confusion." (*BYAA*)

Interval: 5 minutes

"Mindful breathing, mindful walking."(*AWFCF*) Mindful sitting.

3 bells

Conclude

Session 25

Readers note: The next two sessions are taken almost exclusively from poems by Mary Oliver. Both appear in the collection *Dream Work*. The first poem is entitled *Poem*. The only element of the session that is not derived from Oliver is the opening and closing *gatha* for calling attention—back—to one's breathing .

Commence

1 bell

"Just to live is holy." (*IAW*) Come Holy, Come Holy Spirit,

1 bell

Come holy breathing"

1 bell

Come Spirit

Interval: 5 minutes

[**Readers' note:** Employ the poem, "Poem," for the remainder of the session, creating your own intervals.]

Poem

The spirit
  likes to dress up like this:
  ten fingers,
  ten toes,

shoulders, and all the rest
   at night
   in the black branches,
   in the morning

in the blue branches
   of the world.
   It could float, of course,
   but would rather

plumb rough matter.
   Airy and shapeless thing,
   it needs
   the metaphor of the body,

lime and appetite,
   the oceanic fluids;
   it needs the body's world,
   instinct

and imagination
   and the dark hug of time,
   sweetness
   and intelligibility,

to be understood,
   to be more than pure light
   that burns
   where no one is—

so it enters us—
   in the morning
   shines from brut comfort
   like a stitch of lightning;

and at night
   lights up the deep and wondrous
   drownings of the body
   like a star.

Come Holy Spirit.
3 bells

Conclude

Session 26

Commence

1 bell

"I am breathing in and liberating my mind, I am breathing out and liberating my mind."(***BYAA***)
1 bell

"I am breathing in and observing liberation. I am breathing out and observing liberation."(***BYAA***)
1 bell

Interval: 5 minutes

> [**Reader's note:** Employ the poem "Morning Poem" for
> the rest of the session, creating your own intervals].

Morning Poem

Every morning
the world
is created.
Under the orange

sticks of the sun
the heaped
ashes of the night
turn into leaves again

and fasten themselves to the high branches—
and the ponds appear

like black cloth
on which are painted islands

of summer lilies. If it is your nature
to be happy
you will swim away along the soft trails

for hours, your imagination
alighting everywhere.
And if your spirit carries within it

the thorn
that is heavier than lead—
if it's all you can do
to keep on trudging—

there is still
somewhere deep within you
a beast shouting that the earth
is exactly what it wanted—

each pond with its blazing lilies
is a prayer heard and answered
lavishly,
every morning,

whether or not
you have ever dared to be happy,
whether or not
you have ever dared to pray.

"I am breathing in and observing letting go. I am breathing out and observing letting go. This is how we practice." (**BYAA**)

3 bells

Conclude

Session 27

Commence

3 bells

"The chatter of our fears, our anger, our anxiety falls away in serenity; companions, together let us enter through the door of serenity the silence of our hearts." (**WOH**)

Interval: 5 minutes

"There is story of a woman running away from tigers. She runs and runs, and the tigers are getting closer and closer. When she comes to the edge of a cliff, she sees some vines there, so she climbs down and holds onto the vines. Looking down she sees that there are tigers below her as well. She then notices that a mouse is gnawing away at the vine to which she is clinging. She also sees a beautiful little bunch of strawberries close to her, growing out of a clump of grass. She looks up and she looks down. She looks at the mouse. Then she just takes a strawberry, puts it in her mouth, and enjoys it thoroughly." (**WNEPLK**)

Interval: 5 minutes

"In God I trust; I am not afraid. What can a mere mortal do to me?" (Ps 56:11) "I sought the Holy One and was answered and delivered from all my fears." (Ps 34:4) The word of the Holy One came to Abram and said 'do not be afraid, I am your shield.'" (Gen 15:11) "Why are you afraid? Have you still no faith?" (Mark 4:40)

Interval: 5 minutes

"Do not fear anyone unless they can kill your own true self. Aren't two sparrow sold for a penny? Yet not one of them will fall to the ground that the Holy One does not mark it. And even the hairs of your head are all counted. So do not be afraid. You are more valuable than many sparrows." (Mark 10: 28–31)

Interval: 5 minutes

Let us eat our strawberry. "It is gratefulness that makes the soul great." (*IAW*)
3 bells

Conclude

Session 28

Commence

3 bells

"I am breathing in and feeling joyful, breathing out and feeling joyful. (Pause) Those who practice meditation should know how to nourish themselves on the peace and joy of meditative concentration, in order to reach real maturity and help the world." (**BYAA**)

1 bell

Interval: 3 minutes

"Brothers and Sisters, it is now time to recite the Five Wonderful Precepts. Brothers and Sisters, please listen. The Five Precepts are the basis for a happy life. They have the capacity to protect life, and make it beautiful and worth living. They are also the door that opens to enlightenment and liberation. The Fourth Precept.[1] Aware of the suffering caused by unmindful speech and the inability to listen to others, I vow to cultivate loving speech and deep listening in order to bring joy and happiness to others and relieve others of their suffering. Knowing that words can create happiness or suffering, I vow to learn to speak truthfully, using words that inspire self-confidence, joy, and hope. I am determined not to spread news that I do not know to be certain and not to criticize or condemn things of which I am not sure. I will refrain from uttering words that can cause division or discord, or that can cause the family or the community to break. I will make all efforts to reconcile and resolve all conflicts, however small.

---

1. In a group session one may wish to begin this *gatha* with the sentence beginning "Aware."

(Pause) This is the fourth of the Five Precepts. Will you make an effort to study and practice it?" (*BL*)

Interval: 10 minutes

"Incline your heart's ear in obedience to the speech a day makes for your salvation. The first moment of this obedience is to be present to the new day by waiting in silent receptivity until the day speaks its 'word' to you."(*YWTM*).[2]

Interval: 5 minutes

"Let your speech be gentle, serious, modest, brief, and reasonable."(*RB*) "Be still and know that I am God." (Ps 46:10)

Interval: 5 minutes

"I am breathing in and feeling happy, breathing out and feeling happy. Only if we have peace ourselves can we share peace with others." (*BYAA*)

1 bell

Conclude

---

2. Jonathan Montaldo is describing what he takes to be Thomas Merton's great spiritual capacity.

Session 29

Note to readers: This is an Easter mediation session.

Commence

3 bells

"The theological ground of contemplation is the revelation that Christ is risen and is living in us."(**SR**)
1 bell

Interval: 3 minutes

"There is a movement of meditation expressing itself in the paschal rhythm of the Christian life, the passage from death to life in Christ. The end of helplessness, frustration, infidelity, confusion and ignorance." (**CP**)

Interval: 5 minutes

"The grace of Easter is a great silence, and immense tranquility and a clean taste in the soul. It is the taste of heaven. Tasting it for a moment, we are briefly able to see and live all things according to their truth, to possess them in their abundance hidden in God, beyond all sense." (**YWTM**) "Let him easter in us, be a dayspring for the dullness of us, be for us a crimson cresseted east." (**GG**)

Interval: 5 minutes

"If the Risen Christ would always shine in my heart and all around me and before me in His Easter simplicity! For his simplicity is our feast. This the unleavened bread which is manna, this Easter cleanness, this freedom, this sincerity." (**YWTM**)

Interval: 5 minutes

"Rejoice in God always, again I say it rejoice. Let your gentleness be known to everyone. The Holy One is near. Do not worry about anything, but in everything by prayer and supplication with thanksgiving let your request be made know to God. Then the peace of God, which surpasses all understanding, will guard your hearts and minds in Christ Jesus." (Phil 4:4–14)

Interval: 5 minutes

"The grace of Easter . . . see[ing] all things according to their truth." (*YWTM*)

3 bells

Conclude

Session 30

Commence

3 bells

"Return to reality and what is ordinary in silence; it is always there if you know to return to it. The non-ordinary, the tension of meeting people, of discussion, of ideas, these too are good and real, but illusion gets in to them, the unimportant becomes important, words and images become more important than life." (*YWTM*) "Return to reality and what is ordinary in silence."

Interval: 5 minutes

"In active contemplation, a person becomes able to live with themselves. They learn to be at home with their own thoughts. They become to a greater and greater degree independent of exterior supports, peaceful not by passive dependence on things outside themselves—diversions, entertainments, conversations, business—but they derive inner satisfaction from spiritual creativeness: thinking their own thoughts, reaching their own conclusions, looking at their own lives and directing them in accordance with their own inner truth." (*IM*)

Interval: 5 minutes

"If you penetrate by detachment and purity of heart to the inner secret core of you own being, you attain a liberation that no one can touch." (*AJ*)

Interval: 5 minutes

"The only true joy in life is to escape the prison of our own false self and enter by Love into the Life Who lives and sings in the essence of every creature, in the core of our own souls." (*NSC*)

Interval: 5 minutes

"Christ came on earth to form contemplatives." (*CP*)

3 bells

Conclude

Session 31

Commence

3 bells

"Call it Being, call it *Atman*, call it *Pneuma* or Silence and the simple fact that by being attentive, by learning to listen (or by recovering the natural capacity to listen which cannot be taught any more than breathing), we can find ourselves engulfed in such happiness that it cannot be explained: the happiness of being at one with everything in that hidden ground of Love for which there can be no explanation." (*TMLL*)

Interval: 7 minutes

"The function of diversion is to anesthetize people and to plunge them into the warm, apathetic stupor of a collectivity which, like themselves, wishes to remain amused." (*DQ*) "Futile? Life is not futile if you simply live it. It remains futile as long as you keep watching yourself live it; making sure that one has company, that one is justified by the presence and support of others." (*LL*)

Interval: 7 minutes

"In active contemplation, a person thinks their own thoughts and reaches their own conclusions, looking at their own life and directing it in accordance with their own inner truth, discovered in meditation and under the eyes of God. They discover the secret of life in the creative energy of love—not love as a sentimental indulgence, but as a profound and self-giving expression of freedom." (*TIE*)

Interval: 7 minutes

"The best thing I can give to others is to liberate myself from the common delusions and be, for myself and for others, free. Then grace can work in and through me for everyone." (***YWTM***)

Interval: 3 minutes

3 bells

Conclude

Session 32

Commence

1 bell

"No matter how simple discourse may be, it is never simple enough. No matter how simple thought may be, it is never simple enough. No matter how simple love may be, it is never simple enough. The only thing left is the simplicity of the soul in God or, better, the simplicity of God." (**YWTM**).

1 bell

"Either you look at the universe as a very poor creation out of which no one can make anything, or you look at your own life and your own part in the universe as infinitely rich, full of inexhaustible interest opening out into the infinite possibilities for study, for contemplation and interest and praise. Beyond all and in all there is God." (**IM**)

1 bell

Interval: 10 minutes

"From moment to moment, I remember with surprise that I am satisfied, even though everything is not yet fulfilled. To know and to taste the secret good that is present but is not known to those who, because they are restless and because they are discontent and because they complain, cannot apprehend it. The present good—reality—God. *Gustatae et videte*—Taste and see." (**YWTM**)

Interval: 7 minutes

"Those most basic human values which the world most desperately needs to regain: personal integrity, inner peace, authenticity, identity, inner depth, spiritual joy, the capacity to love, the capacity to enjoy God's creation and give thanks." (*CWA*)

Interval: 5 minutes

3 bells

Conclude

Session 33

Commence

1 bell

"The spiritual life is the life of a person's real self, the life of that interior self whose flame is so often allowed to be smothered under the ashes of anxiety and futile concern." (***NMI***)

1 bell

"If you want to have a spiritual life you must unify your life. A life is either all spiritual or not spiritual at all." (***TS***)

1 bell

Interval: 5 minutes

"No one who seeks liberation in light and solitude, no one who seeks spiritual freedom, can afford to yield passively to all the appeals of salesmen, advertisers and consumers. Keep your eyes clean and your ears quiet and your mind serene. Meanwhile keep your sense of compassion for women and men who have forgotten the very concept of solitude." (***NSC***)

Interval: 7 minutes

"All men and women seek peace first of all within themselves. We have to learn to commune with ourselves before we can commune with others and with God. Someone who is not at peace with themselves necessarily projects their interior fighting into the society of those they live with, and spreads a contagion of conflict all around them." (***NMI***)

Interval: 5 minutes

"No one can serve two masters. Your life is shaped by the ends you live for. You are made in the image of what you desire." (*TS*)

Interval: 5 minutes

"The spiritual life is, then, first of all a matter of keeping awake." (*TS*)

1 bell

Conclude

Session 34

Commence

1 bell

"The truest solitude is not something outside you, not an absence of people or of sound around you: it is an abyss opening to the center of your own soul." (*NSC*)

1 bell

This solitude "is clothed in the friendly communion of silence, and this silence is related to love for silence teaches us to know reality by respecting it where words have defiled it." (*TS*)

1 bell

Interval: 5 minutes

"Humans have lost the courage and the faith without which they are not content to be 'unseen.' We are pitifully dependent on self-observation and self-assertion That is to say utterly exiled from God and from our own true selves." (*TIE*)

Interval: 5 minutes

"The only true joy on earth is to escape the prison of our own false self And enter by love into union with the Life Who dwells and sings within the Essence of every creature and in the core of our own souls." (*NSC*)

Interval: 5 minutes

". . . the simple fact that by being attentive, by learning to listen (or recovering the natural capacity to listen which cannot be learned any more than breathing), we can find ourselves engulfed in such happiness that it cannot be explained: the happiness of being at one with everything in that hidden ground of Love for which there can be no explanation." (***THGL***)

Interval: 5 minutes

Be attentive; learn to listen, breathe.

1 bell

Conclude

Session 35

Reader's note: This session is taken exclusively from the writings of the early Sufi master, Mansur Al-Hallaj, the Persian master who lived from 858 till 920 CE. The writing is *Muqatta'at*, **MA**.

Commence.

3 bells

"Where is your place in my heart, Oh God? It is all of my heart. Nothing else besides You has any place in my heart. I saw my Lord[1] with my heart's eye and said: 'Who are you Lord?' 'I am you' God responded."

Interval: 7 minutes

"And *where* is the *where* of you my Lord? The mind conceives nothing like you which would allow it to draw near to where you are. But You indeed encompass every place and even beyond all places. Where then are You God in Yourself? Are you an I and a Thou? That would make two gods! One Selfhood is there, Yours for ever at the heart of my nothingness."

Interval: 7 minutes

"Where then, outside of me, is Your Being, that I may gaze on You as You are? Ah! Already my being dissolves in Your light—no longer has it any place at all. So where again to find Your Face, doubly the object of my desire? Should I image you in my heart—or in my eye?"

---

1. The language, not the content, of this excerpt from the writings of Al-Hallaj is revised significantly. But removing the term *Lord* in Sufi writing would be to falsify it.

Interval: 7 minutes

"I saw my Lord with my heart's eye and said 'Who are you Lord?'
'I am you' said God."

3 bells

Conclude

Session 36

Commence

1 bell

"Composed, body at ease, its breathing regular, the *yoga*, the *yogini* sits absorbed in contemplation. Suddenly a door creaks, a sliver of moonlight shimmers on the ground ahead, a mosquito whines, and they are back in the world." (**RW**)

1 bell

Restless the mind is,
So strongly shaken
In the grip of the senses.
Truly I think
The wind is no wilder. (**BG**)

1 bell

Interval: 5 minutes

"All of us dwell on the brink of the infinite ocean of life's creative power. We carry it within us: supreme strength, the fullness of wisdom, unquenchable joy. It is never thwarted and cannot be destroyed. But it is hidden deep, which makes life a problem. The infinite is down in the darkest, profoundest vault of our being, in the forgotten well-house, the deep cistern." (**RW**)

Interval: 5 minutes

"Body, life, mind, understanding, joy, such things cannot be the true self. They are impermanent, they keep changing, they depend on other realities, and so they cannot be the true, fundamental self which is always utterly simple and free. To realize this is the fruit of discrimination; layers of non-self are peeled away each revealed to be empty, nothing inside it but another empty formulation of identity." (**HWFAGC**)

Interval: 5 minutes

"By seeing what the self is not, ignorance is stripped bare of its disguises. An honest clear look at ourselves confirms the deep roots and pervasiveness of confusion and the futility of the claims we habitually make about being ourselves, improving ourselves, finding ourselves." (**HWFAGC**)

Interval: 5 minutes

"The illumined sage whose only pleasure is in the self ever lives at ease, whether going or staying, sitting or lying down. Satisfied, they possess undiluted bliss, neither grieved nor elated by sense objects, neither attached nor adverse to them. As a child plays with its toys forgetting hunger and bodily pain, exactly so does the person of realization take pleasure in reality, without thought of 'I' or 'mine,' and is happy." (**CJD**)

Interval: 4 minutes

"Composed, body at ease, its breathing regular, the *yogi,* the *yogini,* sits absorbed in meditation." (**RW**)

1 bell

Conclude

Session 37

Note to the reader: All elements of guidedness in this meditation are taken from Saint Augustine.

Commence

3 bells

"I was outside myself, you were inside me. I was a problem to myself." (***CSA***) (Pause) "Descend into yourself. Go into the inner recesses of your mind. If you are far from yourself how can you be near God." (*Sermon 52*)

3 bells

Interval: 7 minutes

"Let us leave a little room for reflection, room too for silence. Enter into yourself and leave behind all noise and confusion. Look within yourself. See if there be some delightful place in your consciousness where you can be free of noise and argument, where you need not be carrying on your disputes and planning to have you own stubborn way. Hear the word in quietness, that you may understand it." (*Sermon 52*)

Interval: 7 minutes

"What is it that I love when I love you? . . . A kind of light, a kind of voice, a certain fragrance, and an embrace, when I love my God: a light, voice, fragrance, food and embrace of my inmost self, where something limited to no place shines into my mind, where something not snatched away by passing time sings for me, where something no breath blows away yields to me its scent, where there is savor undiminished by famished eating, and where I am clasped into a union of which no satiety can tear me away. This is what I love when I love my God." (**CSA**)

Interval: 7 minutes

"Let peace glow in you so as to kindle others." (*Sermon 352*)

3 bells

Conclude

Session 38

Commence

3 bells

"Those who practice meditation should know how to nourish themselves on the peace and joy of meditative concentration, in order to reach real maturity and help the world. Life in this world is both painful and miraculous. Practicing meditation is to be aware of both what is painful and what is miraculous." (**BYAA**)

3 bells

Interval: 7 minutes

"Weather is happening—delightful sunshine, dull sky, or destructive storm—this is undeniable. But if we think we are the weather happening on Mount Zion then the fundamental truth of our union with God remains obscured, and our sense of painful alienation heightened. When the mind is brought to stillness we see that we are the mountain and not the changing patterns of weather appearing on the mountain." (**ISL**)

Interval: 7 minutes

"It is said that your view and your posture should be like a mountain. Sit then, as if you were a mountain, with the unshakable, steadfast majesty of a mountain. A mountain is completely natural and at ease with itself, however strong the winds that batter it, however thick the dark clouds that swirl around its peak. Sitting like a mountain, let your mind rise and fly and soar." (**TBLD**)

Interval: 7 minutes

"God does not know how to be absent." (***ISL***)

3 bells

Conclude

Session 39

Commence

1 bell

" . . . God is not all
In one place complete
. . . God is in the bits and pieces of everyday
A kiss here and a laugh again
And sometimes tears."[1] (**WMUC**)

1 bell

Interval: 1 minute

"Earth is crammed with heaven,
And every common bush afire with God;
But only he who sees takes off his shoes—
The rest sit around and pluck blackberries."[2] (**WMUC**)

1 bell

Interval: 5 minutes

"Spiritual activity that develops its hidden powers of action: the perception of beauty. We ought to be alive enough to reality to see beauty all around us. Beauty is simply reality itself, perceived in a special way that gives it resplendent value of its own." (**NMI**)

Interval: 5 minutes

---

1. Patrick Kavanagh, cited by Thomas H. Groome.
2. Elizabeth Barrett Browning, cited by Thomas H. Groome.

"All who are sensitive to beauty know the almost agonizing sense of revelation its sudden impact brings—the abrupt disclosure of the mountain summit, the wild cherry tree in blossom, the crowning moment of a great concerto, witnessing to another beauty beyond sense. Creation is the activity of an artist possessed by the vision of perfection, who by means of the raw material with which they work, tries to give more perfect expression to their idea, their inspiration, their love. Each human person is an unfinished product, on which the Creative Spirit is always at work." (*SL*)

Interval: 5 minutes

"The world will be saved by beauty." (*TI*)

1 bell

"Out of the silence at the beginning of time
you spoke the word of life.
Out of the world's primeval darkness
you flooded the universe with light.
In the quiet of this place
in the dark of the night
I wait and watch.
In the stillness of my soul
and from its fathomless depths
the senses of my heart are awake to you.
For fresh soundings of life
for new showings of light
I search in the silence of my spirit, Holy One." (*CB*)

Interval: 5 minutes

"The world will be saved by beauty." (*TI*)

Conclude

Session 40

Commence

3 bells

"Regards to the day, the great long day
That can't be hoarded, good or ill.
What breathes us likely means us well." (**BKCBCOA**)

3 bells

Interval: 7 minutes

"Freedom is the basic condition for you to touch life, to touch the blue sky, the trees, the birds, the tea, and the other person. This is why mindfulness practice is very important. Train yourself to drink your tea mindfully, to become a free person while drinking tea. Train yourself to be a free person while you make breakfast." (**AWFCF**)

Interval: 7 minutes

"Many are avidly seeking but they alone find who remain in silence. Every person who delights in a multitude of words, even though they say admirable things, is empty within. If you love truth be a lover of silence. Silence like the sunlight will illumine you in God and will deliver you from the phantoms of ignorance. Silence will unite you to God." (**CP**—Quoting Isaac of Nineveh)

Interval: 7 minutes

"Rejoice in God always, again I say rejoice. Let your gentleness be known to everyone. The Holy One is near. Do not worry about anything, but in everything by prayer and supplication with thanksgiving let your request be made know to God. Then the peace of God, which surpasses all understanding, will guard your hearts and minds in Christ Jesus." (Phil 4: 4–7)

Interval: 1 minute

"Regards to the day, the great long day
That can't be hoarded, good or ill.
What breathes us likely means us well." (**BKCBCOA**)

3 bells

Conclude

Session 41

Commence

3 bells

"We rise from an earthly root
To seek the blossom of the heart.
What breathes us likely means us well." (***BKCBCOA***)

Interval: 6 minutes

"Let a person put away anger and forsake pride. No sufferings befall the one who is not sunk in self, and who calls nothing their own. Those who hold back anger are real chariot drivers; others are but holding the reins. Overcome anger by mildness."(***D***)

Interval: 6 minutes

"Beware the anger of the tongue. Beware the anger of the mind. The steadfast who control body, tongue, and mind are indeed well controlled." (***D***)

Interval: 6 minutes

"Let us live happily, not hating anyone. Let us live happily free from ailments. Let us live happily free from greed. Let us live happily, then, calling nothing our own." (***D***)

Interval: 6 minutes

"We rise from an earthly root
To seek the blossom of the heart.
What breathes us likely means us well." (***BKCBCOA***)

3 bells

Conclude

Session 42

3 bells

"We are a voice impelled to tell
where the joining of sound and silence is.
We need the tides, and their witnesses.
What breathes us likely means us well." (**BKCBCOA**)

Interval: 5 minutes

"Let us live happily, not hating, dwelling free of hating. Let us live happily, free from greed, dwelling free of greed. Let us live happily though we call nothing our own! We shall be like the bright gods, feeding on happiness." (**D**)

Interval: 5 minutes

"Health is the greatest of blessings, contentedness the best riches; trust is the best of relationships. *Nirvana* the highest happiness. Those who taste the sweetness of solitude and tranquility, are free from fear and sin. Follow the wise, the intelligent, the learned, the much enduring, the dutiful, the noble; follow good and wise people as the moon follows the path of the stars." (**D**)

Interval: 5 minutes

"When you practice *zazen*, your mind should be concentrated on your breathing, the fundamental activity of the universal being; without this experience it is impossible to attain absolute freedom. But to concentrate your mind on something is not the true purpose of *Zen*. The true purpose is to see things as they are, to observe things as they are, and to let everything go as it goes; to open small mind, to realize big mind. The rules of practice, keeping your mind on your breathing and your body in the right posture, should become more subtle and careful to experience the vital freedom of *Zen*." (**ZMBM**)

Interval: 5 minutes

"We are a voice impelled to tell
where the joining of sound and silence is.
We are the tides, and their witnesses.
What breathes us likely means us well." (**BKCBCOA**)

Interval: 3 minutes

3 bells

Conclude

Session 43

Commence

3 bells

"The human mind is always looking for possessions and never feels fulfilled. This causes impure actions ever to increase. *Bodhisttvahs* however always remembers the principle of having few desires. They live a simply life in peace in order to practice the Way, and consider the realization of perfect understanding to be their only career." (**SROGB**)

Interval: 5 minutes

"Living the ordinary life extraordinarily well, beyond the superficial and uncaring; to live calmly in the midst of chaos, productively in an arena of waste, lovingly in a maelstrom of individualism, gently in a world full of violence." (**WDDLRB**)

Interval: 5 minutes

"What is necessary, after all, is only this: solitude, vast inner solitude. To walk inside yourself and meet no one for hours—that is what you must be able to obtain. To be solitary as you were when you were a child, when the grown-ups walked around involved with matters that seemed large and important because they looked so busy and because you didn't understand a thing about what they were doing." (**LYP**)

Interval: 5 minutes

"Throughout my life, by means of my life, the world has little by little caught fire in my sight until aflame all around me, it has become luminous from within. Such has been my experience in contact with the earth—the diaphony of the Divine at the heart of a universe on fire." (**CMTLLTA**)

Interval: 5 minutes

"Calmly in the middle of chaos." (**WDDLRB**)

1 bell

"Solitude, vast inner solitude."

1 bell

"Luminous from within."

Conclude

Session 44

Commence

1 bell

"Usually we think 'Now *zazen* meditation is over, and we will go about our everyday activity.' But this is not the right understanding. They are the same thing. We have no where to escape. In activity there is calmness, and in calmness there should be activity. Calmness and activity are not different." (**ZMBM**)

1 bell

"It is the readiness of the mind that is wisdom." (**ZMBM**)

1 bell

Interval: 5 minutes

"May we[1] be peaceful, happy, and light in body and spirit. May we be free from injury, may we live in safety. May we be free from disturbance, fear, anxiety, and worry." (**NP**)

Interval: 5 minutes

"May we learn to look at ourselves with the eyes of understanding and love. May we be able to recognize and touch the seeds of joy and happiness in ourselves. May we learn to identify and see the sources of anger, craving, and delusion in ourselves." (**NP**)

---

1. In his introduction to the posthumously published *Contemplative Prayer* by Thomas Merton, Thich Nhat Hanh composed "The Nine Prayers." Hanh repeats every petition for a) oneself, b) those whom we love, and c) "the one we suffer when we think of." Here all three are reduced to "we," or "ourselves."

Interval: 5 minutes

"May we know how to nourish the seeds of joy in ourselves every day. May we be able to live fresh, solid, and free. May we be free of attachment and aversion, but not be indifferent." (**NP**)

Interval: 5 minutes.

"Calmness and activity are not different. It is the readiness of the mind that is wisdom." (***ZMBM***)

3 bells

Conclude

Session 45

Commence

1 bell

Breathe and practice purity of heart. "Childlike simplicity." (***PHC***)[1]

1 bell

"Clarity of purpose." (***PHC***)

1 bell

"And fine moral discrimination: purity of heart." (***PHC***)

Interval: 5 minutes

"Who shall climb the mountain of God, who shall stand in the holy place? The man or woman of clean hands and pure heart who does not lift up their souls to what is false." (Ps 24:3–4)

Interval: 5 minutes

"Insight into emptiness is the essential Buddhist contribution to the universal wisdom about purity of heart. It frees us from mental afflictions and the actions they give rise to. We feel better and so we act better. Emptiness dispels ignorance and opens awareness. As Jesus looked deep into his own emptiness on the eve of his death and communicated what he felt to his disciples, it was joy."[2] (***PHC***)

Interval: 5 minutes

---

1. All of the quotes from the anthology *Purity of Heart and Contemplation* are authored by Laurence Freeman, OSB.

2. Freeman is citing the Gospel of John 15:11.

"Create in me a clean heart, a heart humble and repentant." (Ps 51)

Interval: 5 minutes

"At the center of our being is a point or spark which belongs entirely to God, which is never at our disposal, from which God disposes our lives. This little point of nothingness and *absolutely poverty* is the pure glory of God in us." (**CGB**)

1 bell

Breathe and practice purity of heart: "childlike simplicity, clarity of purpose, and fine moral discrimination." (**PHC**)

1 bell

Conclude

Session 46

Note to the reader: All the elements of this meditation are taken from the writings, including the poetry, of Robert Lax, Thomas Merton's best friend. Lax became a great minimalist poet and lived the second half of his long life as a hermit on various Greek islands. The opening element of "guidedness" in this session is an untitled poem of Lax's. After the meditation, *the poem is repeated in precisely the manner Lax wrote it.* All quotations are taken from Michael N. McGregor's superb biography of Lax, *Pure Act: The Uncommon Life of Robert Lax.*

Commence

3 bells

"Peace begins when any two beings in the universe attempt (and persevere in trying) to understand each other." (**PA**)

Interval: 3 minutes

"Maybe a good life can be lived quietly, maybe a guy with a good idea doesn't have to be particularly brave about presenting it, maybe work on it quietly all his life and live it for a heritage." (**PA**)

Interval: 3 minutes

"This just occurred to me. My idea of a good contemplative is something more like a cow than it is a dancing master, healthy, calm and peaceful in spirit. If you're calm and peaceful and healthy and see things clearly, you're there to help whoever needs you, and you're able to do whatever has to be done." (**PA**)

Interval: 5 minutes

"Taking dictation from an angel is meaningless as a human activity; it could be done by a robot. Listening to one's inner voice is different: when the inner voice is heard, it is recognized as the speaker's own." (*PA*)

(Pause)

"Each moment should have the power of an instinctive movement, but should be fully informed by thought—a combination of reflection and spontaneity; a response, an immediate response to stimulus: immediate but total and mature." (*PA*)

Interval: 10 minutes

"Peace begins when any two beings in the universe attempt (and persevere in trying) to understand each other." (*PA*)

1 bell

Conclude

peace
be
gins

when
an
y
two
be
ings

in
the
un
i
verse
at
tempt

(&
per
se
vere

in
try
ing)

to
un
der
stand

each
oth
er

–

Session 47

Commence

1 bell

We begin by renewing our friendship with our breath.

1 bell

We begin by renewing our intimacy with our breath.

1 bell

We begin by renewing our identity with our breath.

Interval: 5 minutes

"Salvation is first of all the full discovery of who one really is."
(*NMI*) "To be 'lost' is to be left to the pretenses of the ego. To be
'saved' is to return to one's inviolate and eternal reality and to live
in God." (*NSC*)

Interval: 5 minutes

Salvation: "an actual human change, a gradual transformation
from natural self-centeredness to a radical new orientation centered in God and manifest in the fruits of the Holy Spirit," [love,
joy, peace, patience, kindness, generosity, faithfulness, gentleness,
self-control.] (Gal 5:22–23) (*MTOW*)

Interval: 5 minutes

"Song in our silence, light in our darkness, waters of life for our
thirst. You are the freshness of birth every morning, the grace that
encircles our day." (*SIOS*)

Interval: 5 minutes

We conclude by renewing our friendship with our breath.

1 bell

We conclude by renewing our intimacy with our breath.

1 bell

We conclude by renewing our identity with our breath.

1 bell

Conclude

Session 48

Commence

1 bell

"We breathe to empty our inner life of the 'separate self sense.'"[1] (**FCP**)

1 bell

We breathe to empty our inner lives of everything we fill them with: "fears, reflections, regrets, anxiety" (**ADP**), futile concerns, worry, discontent, restlessness, complaining, resentment; "routine, confused, chaotic, and self-serving activities of the false self," (**TIE**), obsessed with what is "extrinsic, transient, illusory and trivial" (**NMI**), feeling "helplessness, frustration, infidelity, confusion and ignorance." (**CP**)

1 bell

We breathe to experience that we are empty of isolated self and full of one another, and of "the sky, the clouds, the rain, the sunshine, the earth." (**HU**)

1 bell

Interval: 5 minutes

"Body[2] is emptiness, emptiness is body. Body does not differ from emptiness, nor does emptiness differ from body. The same is true

1. The source of sin in the world for Thomas Keating, OCSO.

2. This is the defining *gatha* inside the *Prajna Paramitar Sutra, The Heart of Understanding Sutra*, among the greatest Scriptures in all Buddhism. In the sutra, "body" is referred to as "form," one of five "bunches" or aggregates, in

of feelings, perceptions, mental formations and consciousness."
(*HU*) All are empty; peacefully, refreshingly . . . Empty!

Interval: 5 minutes

"We should treat our anxiety, our pain, our hatred and passion
gently, respectfully, not resisting it but living with it, making peace
with it, penetrating into its nature by meditation on interdependence." (*MM*)

Interval: 5 minutes

"Gone, gone, gone all the way—everyone gone over, everyone gone
to the other shore—enlightenment. *Svaha.*"[3] (*HU*)

Interval: 5 minutes

"Every event, every moment plants seeds in a person's life.

We are at liberty to be false or to be true

To be real or unreal." (*NSC*)

3 bells

Conclude

Sanskrit *Skandahs*, that constitute a person: form, feeling, perception, mental
formations, and consciousness.

3. *Svaha:* "cry of joy or excitement, like 'welcome!' or 'Hallelujah.'" (*HU*)

Session 49

Commence

3 bells

"Hold your being secure and quiet. Keep your life collected in its own center. Do not allow your thoughts to be disturbed." (***WCT***)

Interval: 5 minutes

"God and our true self are not separate." (***FCP***) "God is your being, and what you are you are in God." (***CU***) God is "like a great tree spread out over me with love in every limb." (***CMTLLTA***)[1] God is "the highest wisdom and the most radiant beauty." (***WAISI***)

Interval: 5 minutes

God "is found where you hide yourself in the secret place of your heart, in the quiet solitude where no word is spoken." (***CP***) "We recollect ourselves and enter into the temple (our inner self) in which, in all truth we find God dwelling and at work. And we taste God and enjoy God like something that springs from the ground not from a cistern." (***CP***)[2]

Interval: 5 minutes

"In allowing God to work in it, the soul is at once illumined and transformed in God and God communicates to it supernatural being in such a way that all things of God and the soul are one in participant transformation . . ." (***CP***)[3]

---

1. Quoting Hildegard of Bingen.
2. Quoting Johannes Tauler.
3. Quoting John of the Cross.

Interval: 5 minutes

"God has given to the earth the breath which feeds it. It is God's breath that gives life to all things. It is the breath of God that you breathe." (*TBOA*)

Interval: 2 minutes

"God is your being." (*CU*)

Conclude

Session 50

Reader's note: Session 50 is Francis of Assisi's *Canticle of Brother Sun and Sister Moon*. It is recommended for near the beginning of spring.

Commence

1 bell

"Most High, all-powerful, all-good Lord, All praise is Yours, all glory, all honor and all blessings."

1 bell

"To you alone Most High do they belong, and no mortal lips are worthy to pronounce Your Name."

1 bell

"Praised be you my Lord with all Your creatures,
Especially Brother Sun,
Who is the day through whom You give us light.
And he is beautiful and radiant with great splendor.
Of You, Most High, he bears the likeness."

Interval: 5 minutes

"Praise be you, my Lord, through Sister Moon and the Stars,
In the heavens you have made them bright, precious and fair."

Praised be You my Lord through
Sister Water,

So useful, humble, precious and
pure.

Praised be You my Lord through
Brother Fire,
Through whom you light the night
and he is beautiful and playful and
robust and strong."

Interval: 5 minutes

"Praised be You my Lord through our
Sister,
Mother Earth
Who sustains and governs us,
Producing varied fruits with colored
flowers and herbs.
Praise be You my Lord through
Those who grant pardon for love of
You and bear sickness and trial.

Blessed are those who endure in
peace, By You Most High, they will be crowned."

Interval: 5 minutes

"Praised be You my Lord through
Sister Death,
from whom no one living can
escape.[1] Blessed are they She finds doing Your Will.
No second death can do them harm."

Interval: 5 minutes

"Praise and bless my
Lord and give God thanks,
And serve God with great humility."

---

1. At this point Francis's prayer then reads, "Woe to those who die in mortal sin."

Interval: 1 minute

"And serve God with great humility."

3 bells

Conclude

Session 51

Reader's note: This meditation is taken entirely from the *Bhaddekaratta Sutta*, "The Sutra on Knowing the Better Way to Live Alone," contained in the translation and commentary on the Buddhist text by Thich Nhat Hanh in the book entitled *Our Appointment with Life: The Buddha's Teaching on Living in the Present* (*OAL*).

Commence

3 bells

The Buddha heard of a forest monk, Thera, who felt the only way to achieve enlightenment was to live alone. He called the monk to come see him in his encampment with many other monks and said "Monk Thera, I want to tell you a way to live alone that is much more enjoyable, much more deep and wonderful."(*OAL*) Then the Buddha said to the monk

"Do not pursue the past
Do not lose yourself in the future.
The past no longer is.
The future has not yet come."

Interval: 5 minutes

"Looking deeply at life as it is
In the very here and now,
The practitioner dwells
In stability and freedom."

Interval: 5 minutes

"We must be vigilant today,
To wait until tomorrow is too late.
Death comes unexpectedly.
How can we bargain with it?"

Interval: 5 minutes

"The sage calls a person who knows
How to dwell in mindfulness
Night and day
'one who knows
The better way to live alone.'"

Interval: 5 minutes

"The practitioner dwells in stability and freedom."

1 bell

Conclude

Session 52

Commence

1 bell

Breathe in and breathe out, gently, calmly, deeply,
gratefully, peacefully.

1 bell

So as to achieve *Bodhicitta*, spontaneous enlightenment mind;
seeking enlightenment "for the benefit of all sentient beings"
(**PHC**). Seeking enlightenment for the sake of compassion.

1 bell

Pause

Shantideva expressed the heart of *Bodhicitta*:

"The source of all misery in the world
Lies in thinking of oneself.
The source of all happiness
Lies in thinking of others." (**PHC**)

Interval: 7 minutes

Contemplation is the attitude of heart required by an interrelated
world view. What the contemplative sees is that center of love in
which all things find their uniqueness. Out of such an experience
we learn to see the face of God in the face of every other human
being and of all creation. (**RTC**)

Interval: 7 minutes

"Contemplation is the way out of the great self-centered psychodrama. When interior silence is discovered, compassion flows. If we deepen our inner silence, our compassion for others is deepened. We cannot pass through the doorways of silence without becoming part of God's embrace of all humanity in its suffering and joy." (**ISL**)

Interval: 7 minutes

"When interior silence is discovered, compassion flows." (**ISL**)

3 bells

Conclude

Session 53

Breath like a flower, fresh![1]

1 bell

Breath like a mountain, solid![2]

1 bell

Breathe and feel still and spacious![3]

1 bell

"A brother asked Abba Poemen, 'What does it means to be angry with your brother without cause?'" Abba answered, 'If your brother hurts you by his arrogance and you are angry with him that is getting angry without a cause. If he hurts you physically and you are angry with him that is getting angry without a cause. But if he cuts you off from God—then you have every right to be angry.'" (**SHC**)

Interval: 5 minutes

"The interior person enters into themselves in a simple manner to apply themselves to a simple gaze in fruitful love. There they encounter God without intermediary. And from the unity of God there shines into them a simple light." (**CP**)[4]

---

1. In essence from **BL**.
2. In essence from **BL**.
3. In essence from **BL**.
4. Quoting John of Ruysbroeck, a fourteenth-century Flemish mystic.

Interval: 7 minutes

"How lovely is your dwelling place, God of hosts. My heart and my soul ring out their joy to God, the living God. They are happy who dwell in your house. They are happy whose strength is in you, in whose hearts are the road to freedom." (Ps 84)[5]

Interval: 10 minutes

Breathe to be fresh, solid, still, and spacious. (*BL*)

3 bells

Conclude

5. The last word of this quote from portions of Psalm 84 is "Zion," not "freedom."

Session 54

1 bell

Practice mindful breathing, mindful walking.[1]

1 bell

Breathe to become free of the past, free of the future, free of your projects.[2]

1 bell

"Christ came to save us from our sins; the source of all sin is the separate self sense. The separate self sense is, of course, the false self. Purity of heart is freedom from the false self system, freedom to be at the disposal of God and those we serve." (**FCP**)[3]

Interval: 8 minutes

"Christ's first word when beginning his ministry, 'repent,' means to change the direction in which we are looking for happiness, the false self's emotional programs for survival and security, affection and esteem, power and control. People who take responsibility for their emotions do not project their painful emotions on other people." (**FCP**)

Interval: 8 minutes

---

1. Paraphrased from *AWFCF*.
2. Paraphrased from *AWFCF*.
3. Also, in part, in Session 48.

"Heart is a term that refers to our innermost depths that ground thought and feeling, our knowing center, is the place of divine encounter." (*ASA*) "God speaks in the great silence of the heart." (*ASA*)[4]

Interval: 8 minutes

Breathe and be free.

3 bells

Conclude

4. Laird, quoting Saint Augustine in this second quote from *ASA*.

Session 55

1 bell

We cannot listen through chatter. We overcome chatter and become aware and attentive through mindful breathing, conscious breathing; listening in the present moment.

1 bell

Learn to listen in the present moment, learn to breathe in, learn to breathe out.

1 bell

Interval: 8 minutes

"The chatter of our fear, our anger, our anxiety; the chatter of our desires and curiosities, of our projected plans and unfinished work falls away in serenity, and makes space, an open space for a new heart, created in the silence of prayer, created in the prayer of silence. A heart that is free, peaceful, quiet and calm, a heart that is one." (**WOH**)

Interval: 8 minutes

"Whatever it is in us that grasps and craves is soothed and calmed and begins to loosen its grip. The inner chatter needs this craving in order to cling. But inner chatter cannot cling to simple awareness. That which sees the chatter arise and fall is free of it." (**ASA**)

Interval: 8 minutes

"The simple fact is that by being attentive, by learning to listen (or recovering the natural capacity for listening which cannot be learned any more than breathing), we can find ourselves engulfed in the happiness of being at one with everything in that hidden ground of Love for which there can be no explanation." (*TMLL*)

Breathe . . . listen . . . happiness.

1 bell

Conclude

Session 56

Commence

3 bells

Come Holy Spirit—Come Holy breath. "God is breath." (*ISL*)[1]

"Happy are the poor in spirit, theirs is the reign of God.[2]
Happy are those who mourn for they will be comforted.
Happy are the gentle for they will inherit the earth."

Interval: 8 minutes

"Happy are those who hunger and thirst for justice; they will be filled.
Happy are the merciful for they will receive mercy.
Happy are the pure of heart for they will see God."

Interval: 8 minutes

"Happy are the peacemakers for they will be called children of God.
Happy are those who are persecuted for justice's sake, for theirs is the reign of heaven.
Happy are you when people revile you on my account."

Interval: 8 minutes

"You are the salt of the earth. You are the light of the world."

3 bells

Conclude

1. Quoting St. Maximus the Confessor.
2. Matt 5:3–14.

Session 57

Commence

1 bell

The bell "calls us back to ourselves."(**BL**)

1 bell

"We should respect this sound, stop thinking and talking, and return to ourselves with breathing and a smile." (**BL**)

1 bell

Aquinas says "unmitigated seriousness betokens a lack of virtue because it wholly despises play, which is as necessary for a good human life as rest." (**MAP**) And Plato: "life should be lived as play." (**OMWH**)

Interval: 8 minutes

"The happily playing child, the virtuoso playing upon their instrument, the genius whose work flows from their fingers with the effortless ease of one playing a game, all these are but realizations of a human being's deep-seated longing for a free, unfettered, eager harmony between body and soul." (**MAP**)

Interval: 8 minutes

"I God am your playmate!
I will lead the child in you in wonderful ways
for I have chosen you."

"Then I shall leap into love—from love into knowledge—from knowledge into enjoyment."[1] (**OMWH**)

Interval: 8 minutes

"I ask God to give you every blessing and joy and to keep ever fresh and young your 'child's mind,' which is the only mind worth having." (**HGL**)

3 bells

Conclude

---

1. Quoting Mechthild of Magdeberg, a thirteenth-century mystic.

Session 58

Commence

1 bell

Only those who breathe mindfully (gently, calmly, deeply, gratefully, peacefully) in the present moment know how to let go. Breathe mindfully.

1 bell

"The Buddha told his monks this story.[1] There was a farmer who had twelve cows and some sesame seed fields. One day his cows all disappeared; he looked everywhere for them, but could not find them. Searching for the lost cows he passed the Buddha teaching his monks, and the farmer said: 'Oh, monks I am the most unhappy man, I think I shall die! I have only twelve cows, and they are all gone, and I don't know what I will do. I think I shall die. And I have seven sesame fields, all eaten by locusts, but mostly my lost cows. I am the most unhappy man; I think I shall die!'"

"And the Buddha told the farmer he didn't see the cows, but maybe the farmer should go look in this direction. And when the man ran off, the Buddha turned to his monks and said this: 'Oh, monks you are very lucky. You have no cows.'"

"So, if you have cows, whether inside or outside, let them go! Your happiness, your capacity to live your life, depends on your capacity to let go your cows."

---

1. This is all taken from a *dharma* talk offered by Thich Nhat Hanh in Berkeley, California, in the summer of 1992, and produced as a DVD, *The Practice of Peace.* (**PP**)

1 bell

Interval: 20 minutes

"If you have cows, whether inside or outside, let them go"!

1 bell

Conclude

Session 59

1 bell

Breathe and "hold your being secure and quiet." (**WCT**)

1 bell

Breathe and "keep your life collected in its own center." (**WCT**)

1 bell

"God is your being, and what you are you are in God." (**CU**)

1 bell

Interval: 5 minutes

"There is no real occasion for tumult, strain, conflict, anxiety once we have reached the living condition that God is all. All takes place with God, God alone matters, God alone is. Our spiritual life is God's affair, because whatever we may think to the contrary, it is really produced by God's steady attraction, and our humble and self-forgetful response to it. It consists in being drawn, at God's pace and in God's way to the place where God wants us to be, not the place we fancied for ourselves." (**SL**)

Interval: 5 minutes

"I the fiery essence, I am aflame beyond the beauty of the meadows. I gleam in the water, I burn in the sun, moon and stars. With every breeze, as with invisible life that contains everything, I awaken everything to life. I am the breeze that nurtures all things green. I encourage blossoms to flourish with ripening fruits. I am the rain from the dew that causes the grasses to laugh with the joy of life."[1] (*CMTLLTA*)

Interval: 10 minutes

"God is your being, and what you are you are God." (*CU*)

Conclude

---

1. Quoting Hildegard of Bingen.

Session 60

Commence

3 bells

The heart pumps air and enables breathing. "Listen with the ear of your heart." (**RB**)

"We must learn to listen to the truths of those around us, and listen to the circumstances of our own lives, what our own life patterns may be saying to us. When we are afraid, what message lurks beyond the fear? Listening and love are clearly of a piece." (**WDDLRB**)

Interval: 7 minutes

Embrace a "spirituality charged with living the ordinary life extraordinarily well: calmly in the middle of chaos, productively in an arena of waste, lovingly in a maelstrom of individualism, gently in a world full of violence." (**WDDLRB**)

Interval: 7 minutes

"Listen with the heart of Christ. Listen with the lover's ear. Listen for the voice of God. Listen in your own heart for the sound of truth." (**WDDLRB**)

Interval: 7 minutes

"Consider the silence of a living tree.
It neither speaks nor hears,
It needs no words,

Yet its presence
Is no less actual than ours." (*U1*)

3 bells

Conclude

Session 61

1 bell

Let us breathe in and out and grow contemplative. "We are built for contemplation, like the rhododendron's capacity to flower, the fledgling's for flight and the child's for self-forgetful abandon and joy." (*ISL*)

1 bell

Humility is "a proper sense of self in a universe of wonders." (*S21stC*)

1 bell

"Humility lies in knowing who we are and what our lives are meant to garner. The irony of humility is that, if we have it, we know we are made for greatness, we are made for God." (*S21stC*)

Interval: 8 minutes

"How does a person seek union with God? The seeker asked. The harder you seek, the teacher said, the more distance you create between God and you. So what does one do about the distance? Understand that it isn't there, the teacher said. Does that mean God and I are one? The seeker said. Not one, not two. How is that possible? the seeker asked. The sun and its light, the ocean and the wave, the singer and the song. Not one, not two." (*S21stC*)

Interval: 10 minutes

"The humble person never uses speech to grind the other person to dust. The humble person cultivates a soul in which everyone is safe. A humble person handles the presence of the other with soft hands, a velvet heart, and an unveiled mind." (*S21stC*)

Interval: 8 minutes

Like the rhododendron, the fledgling, the child (*ISL*); Breathe! "Contemplative prayer is the world in which God can do anything." (*FCP*)

3 bells

Conclude

Session 62

Readers note: With the exception of the word "breathe," this session is taken entirely from Joyce Rupp, "In Praise of Gazing," *National Catholic Reporter*, October 28–November 10, 2011.

Commence

1 bell

"Gazing is the opposite of gawking. Gazing begins with an external look but ends with an internal stirring. Gazing is soul seeing."

1 bell

"When you really look deeply at something, it becomes a part of you."[1]

1 bell

"The reality of oneness we discover in gazing both humbles and exalts us."

Interval: 7 minutes

"In our world of hostility and fear, the peoples of the earth, and the planet itself, cry out for respect, kindness, tenderness. We will have peace only if we learn to gaze rather than gawk at one another."

Interval: 7 minutes

"The beauty of gazing is that we come with an attitude of openness and receptivity. We slow down, pause. This way of looking with

---

1. Quoting John O'Donohue, *Anam Cara: A Book of Celtic Wisdom.*

soft eyes and nonjudgment moves us to a quiet place of respect and awe."

Interval: 7 minutes

Breathe and gaze and practice "soul seeing."

Interval: 1 minute

1 bell

Conclude

Session 63

1 bell

Breathe and return to the present moment.

1 bell

"Dear God I promise you one small thing: I shall never burden my today with cares about tomorrow, although that takes some practice." (*AIL*)

1 bell

"For earth's cycles and seasons
for the rising of spring and the growing summer
for autumn's fullness and the hidden depths of winter
thanks be to you.
For the life force in seeds buried in the ground
that shoot green and bear fruit and fall to the earth
thanks be to you.
Let me learn from earth's cycles of birthing
the time and seasons of dying.
Let me learn of you in the soil of my soul, O Christ,
and your journey from death to birth.
Let me learn of you in my soul
and the journey of letting go." (*CB*)

Interval: 6 minutes

"'My name is I am.' He paused.
I waited. He continued,

'When you live in the past,
with its mistakes and regrets,
It is hard. I am not there.
My name is not I was.'" (**ZSCS**)[1]

Interval: 6 minutes

"On the Sabbath we try to become attuned to *holiness in time*; we are called upon to share in what is eternal in time. Judaism teaches us to be attached to holiness in time." (**IAW**)

Interval: 6 minutes

Breathe and return to the present moment. "My name is I am." (**ZSCS**)

Conclude

---

1. Robert E. Kennedy, SJ, is quoting an anonymous poem; thus the retaining of "He."

Session 64

Commence

1 bell

Holy Spirit, holy breathing. "The Holy Spirit is the direct seizure, the direct grasping of beauty." (***TI***)

1 bell

There is "the fire of divine love and the dazzling brilliance of God's beauty inside everything." (**HBSTM**)

1 bell

Interval: 7 minutes

Dorothy Day: "I look back on my childhood and remember beauty. The smell of sweet clover in a vacant lot, a hopeful clump of grass growing up through the cracks of a city pavement. A feather dropped from some pigeon. A stalking cat. I have always found a strange beauty in the suffering faces which surround us in the city." (***TCW***)

Interval: 7 minutes

"All who are sensitive to beauty know the almost agonizing sense of revelation its sudden impact brings—the abrupt disclosure of the mountain summit, the wild cherry tree in blossom, the crowning moment of a great concerto, witnessing to another beauty beyond sense." (***SL***)

Interval: 7 minutes

"There is a spiritual activity that develops its hidden power of action: the perception of beauty! We ought to be alive enough to reality to see beauty all around us. Beauty is simply reality itself, perceived in a special way that gives it a resplendent value of its own." (*NMI*)

Interval: 7 minutes

"The world will be saved by beauty." (*TI*)

3 bells

Conclude

Session 65

3 bells

"My work is to free myself of myself
So that you can be
born in me." (**MEBH**)

3 bells

"All the communions of a lifetime are one communion. All the communions of women and men now living are one communion. All the communions of all men and women, present, past and future, are one communion." (**SF**).[1]
1 bell

Interval: 7 minutes

"This is the point we must bear in mind: in no case could the cosmos be conceived, and realized, without a supreme center of spiritual consistence."(**SF**)[2]
1 bell

Interval: 7 minutes

"The presence of the Incarnate Word penetrates everything, as a universal element. It shines at the common heart of things, as a center that is infinitely intimate to them and at the same time infinitely distant." (**SF**)[3]

1. Quoting Pierre Teilhard de Chardin, *The Divine Milieux.*
2. Quoting Teilhard, *My Universe.*
3. Quoting Teilhard, *My Universe.*

1 bell

Interval: 8 minutes

"What I cry out for, like every being, with my whole life and all my earthly passions, is something very different from an equal to cherish: it is a God to adore." (*SF*)[4]

Conclude

4. Quoting Teilhard, *The Divine Milieux.*

Session 66

Commence

1 bell

"I am breathing in and liberating my mind; I am breathing out and liberating my mind." (**BYAA**)

1 bell

"I am breathing in and observing liberation; I am breathing out and observing liberation." (**BYAA**)

1 bell

Interval: 10 minutes

"Nothing is more practical than finding God,
than falling in Love in a quite absolute, final way.
What you are in love with, what seizes your
imagination, will affect everything.
It will decide what will get you out of bed in
the morning, what you do with your evenings,
how you spend your weekends,
what you read, whom you know,
what breaks your heart, and
what amazes you with joy and gratitude.
Fall in Love, stay in love,
and it will decide everything."[1] (**ULB**)

Interval: 14 minutes

---

1. Quoting Pedro Aruppe, SJ.

"Down to the place whence springs the I,
Plunge within thyself
Like the diver searching for the pearl." (*SCAAE*)

Conclude

Session 67

Commence

1 bell

We begin by renewing our friendship with our breath.

1 bell

We begin by renewing our intimacy with our breath.

1 bell

We begin by renewing our identity with our breath.

Interval: 10 minutes

"To love is to discover and complete one's self in someone other than oneself, an impossible act so long as each can see in the neighbor no more than a closed fragment following its own course through the world. It is precisely this state of isolation that will end if we begin to discover in each other a single Spirit in search of Itself." (**ULB**)

Interval: 14 minutes

"Plant seeds of peace, joy and understanding in yourself in order to facilitate the work of transformation in the depths of your consciousness." (**FMT**)

Conclude

Session 68

Reader's note: With the exception of the opening *gatha*, everything in this session is from Saint Theresa of Avila's *The Interior Castle*. The opening *gatha* is from Nicephorus the Solitary, a thirteenth-century Orthodox monk.

Commence

3 bells

"Having collected your mind, lead it into the channel of breathing through which air reaches the heart and, together with this inhaled air, allows your mind to descend into the heart and remain there." (*AMPD*)

Interval: 7 minutes

"Prayer in my opinion is nothing else than intimate sharing between friends; it means taking time frequently to be alone with God who we know loves us. (*TIC*)

Interval: 7 minutes

"Let nothing disturb you,
Nothing frighten you.
All things are passing.
God never changes.
Patient endurance gains all things.
Who God possesses
Wants for nothing." (*TIC*)

Interval: 8 minutes

"However quietly we speak, the Holy One is so near that the Holy One will hear us. We need no wings to go in search of God but have only to find a place where we can be alone and look upon the Holy One." (*TIC*)

Conclude

Session 69

Readers note: With the exception of the closing *gatha*, all elements of this session are taken from Thomas Merton's *Thoughts in Solitude*.

Commence

3 bells

"The Spiritual life is, then, first of all a matter of keeping awake. We must not lose our sensitivity to spiritual inspirations."

Interval: 5 minutes

"My Lord God, I have no idea where I am going. I do not see the road ahead of me. I cannot know for certain where it will end. Nor do I really know myself, and the fact that I think I am following your will does not mean that I am actually doing so. But I believe that the desire to please you does in fact please you. And I hope I have the desire in all that I am doing. I hope that I will never do anything apart from that desire. And I know that if I do this you will lead me by the right road, though I may know nothing about it. Therefore I will trust you always though I may seem to be lost and in the shadow of death. I will not fear, for you are ever with me, and you will never leave me to face my peril alone."

Interval: 10 minutes

"To be grateful is to recognize the love of God
in everything. God has given us everything. Every
breath we draw is a gift of God's love, every moment
of existence is a grace. Gratitude therefore takes

nothing for granted. The grateful know that God is good, not by hearsay but by experience."

Interval: 5 minutes

3 bells

Conclude

Session 70

Note to the reader: This session is entirely given over to breathing in and breathing out Christ. My teacher, Gabriel Moran (his memory be a blessing, died October 15, 2021), defended Karl Rahner's famous—some say infamous—term "anonymous Christians." In *Believing in a Revealing God*, Moran reminds the reader of Rahner's words, that the anonymous Christian is "anyone who courageously accepts life [and] . . . who bears patiently with the poverty of the superficial." Rahner himself welcomed being called an "anonymous Buddhist," presumably by someone who noticed that he made the effort to live according to the Four Holy Noble Truths. In other words, Rahner was saying that if your life embodies "love, joy, peace, patience, kindness, generosity, faithfulness, gentleness, self-control," (the "fruit" of the Holy Spirit, according to Paul [Gal 5:22–23]), whatever religion or humanism you are in, *you are living in a way that Christians call "Christian."*

Commence

1 bell

When we follow our breathing, we are already at ease, not dominated by our anxieties and longings.[1] (*TH*)

1 bell

As we breathe consciously, our breath becomes more regular, and peace and joy arise and become more stable with every moment.[2] (*TH*)

---

1. Taken from Session 71 to follow.
2. Taken from Session 71 to follow.

1 bell

Interval: 5 minutes

"We cannot find Christ nature by arduous effort. Reality cannot be caught by thinking or feeling mind. Moment by moment to watch our breathing, to watch our posture, is true nature. There is no secret beyond this point . . . How to sit is how to act." (**ZMBM**)

1 bell

Interval: 5 minutes

"Christ forms Himself through grace and faith in the hearts of those who love him. . . . Therefore if you want to have in your heart the affections and dispositions that were those of Christ on earth . . . [e]nter into the darkness of interior renunciation, strip your self of images and let Christ form himself in you by his cross." (**NSC**)

1 bell

Interval: 5 minutes

"There is a 'movement' of meditation expressing the 'paschal' rhythm of the Christian life, the passage from death to life in Christ . . . the passage from helplessness, frustration, infidelity, confusion and ignorance . . . to life in Christ." (**CP**)

1 bell

Interval: 5 minutes

"Faith in Jesus as the Christ implies we recognize in Jesus our own human-divine self, the self that bears God's image and is alive with God's own breath. This is not belief in something outside ourselves, but existential trust that God's loving presence can be realized in us, and through us, in the world. (**DTW**)

1 bell

Interval: 5 minuets

"Relying on our breathing, we come back to ourselves and are able to restore the oneness of our body and our mind." (*TH*)³

Conclude

> **Second note to the reader.** This "cosmic Christ" is exceptionally well evoked by J. Philip Newell in *Celtic Benediction*.

Blessed are you, O Child of the Dawn,
for your light that dapples through the creation
on leaves that shimmer in the morning sun
and in showers of rain that wash the earth.
Blessed are you
for the human spirit dappled with eternal light
in its longing for love and birth
and its pain-filled passion and tears.
Blessed are you O Christ,
for you awaken me to life.
Blessed are you
for you stir me to true desire. (*CB*)

3. Taken from Session 71 to follow.

Session 71

Note to the reader. As this book approaches its conclusion, this session is given entirely to breathing. It is taken, also in its entirety, from Nhat Hanh's *Transformation and Healing*, a translation and commentary on the *Satipatthana Sutra*, the sutra of the Four Foundations of Mindfulness.

Commence

1 bell

"The first result of conscious breathing is returning to ourselves." (***TH***)

1 bell

Interval: 5 minutes

"In everyday life we often get lost in forgetfulness. Our mind chases after thousands of things, and we rarely take time to come back to ourselves. When we are lost in forgetfulness like that for a long time, we lose touch with ourselves and we feel alienated from ourselves." (***TH***)

1 bell

Interval: 5 minutes

"Another result of conscious breathing is that we come in contact with life in the present moment, the only moment when we can touch life. The life that is in us and around us is wonderful and abundant. If we are not free, we cannot be in contact with it." (***TH***)

1 bell

Interval: 5 minutes

"We should not be imprisoned by regrets about the past, anxieties for the future or attachments or aversions in the present. If we are so imprisoned we are not really living our lives." (*TH*)

1 bell

Interval: 5 minutes

"While the mind is following the breath, the mind *is* the breath. In the process of the practice, our breathing naturally becomes more regular, harmonious, and calm." (*TH*)

1 bell

Interval: 5 minutes

"Coming back to ourselves is already a remarkable success on the path of the practice." (*TH*)

Conclude

Session 72

Readers note: The last word belongs to Evelyn Under-hill, and it is, like the words of Camus, about the end of "winter."

Sisters and brothers, I wish you good meditation

1 bell

Stop
Breathe
Be still

1 bell

Pay attention
Look deeply
Be present

1 bell

Let go
Be empty
Free!

Interval: 10 minutes

"Being, not wanting, having and doing, is the essence of the spiritual life. Our ups and downs, desires, cravings are seen in scale, as small and transitory within a vast abiding spiritual world, lit by a steady spiritual light." (**SL**)

"A spiritual life is simply a life in which all that we do comes from the centre, where we are anchored in God: a life soaked through by a sense of God's reality and claim, and self-given to the great movement of God's will." (**SL**)

Interval: 10 minutes

Those on the "Mystical Way: for them the winter is over: the time of the singing of birds is come. From the deeps of the dewy garden, Life—new and unquenchable—comes to meet them with the dawn." (**M**)

Interval: 3 minutes

1 bell

Sisters and brothers, thank you for meditating with one another and with me.

Bibliography

Chodron, Pema. *The Wisdom of No Escape and the Path of Loving Kindness.* Boston: Shambala, 1991.

Dworkin, Ronald. *Religion without God.* Cambridge: Harvard University Press, 2013.

Einstein, Albert. *The World as I See It.* N.p.: Snowball, 2014 (first published 1935).

Gutierrez, Gustavo. *On Job: God-Talk and the Suffering of the Innocent.* Maryknoll, NY: Orbis, 1987.

Fox, Everett. *The Five Books of Moses: Genesis, Exodus, Leviticus, Numbers, Deuteronomy.* The Shocken Bible 1. New York: Shocken, 2000.

Francis, Pope. *Letter to a Non-Believer.* September 4, 2013. Vatican: Dicastero perla Communicazione Liberia Editrice Vaticana. https://www.vatican.va/content/francesco/en/letters/2013/documents/papa-francesco_20130911_eugenio-scalfari.html.

Hanh, Thich Nhat. *Living Buddha, Living Christ.* New York: Riverhead, 1995.

Heschel, Abraham Joshua. *I Asked for Wonder: A Spiritual Anthology.* Edited by Samuel H. Dresner. New York: Crossroad, 1997. (First published 1983).

Kelley, Joseph T. *Saint Augustine of Hippo: Selections from Confessions and Other Essential Writings Annotated and Explained.* Woodstock, VT: Skylight Paths, 2010.

Kristof, Nicholas. "What Religion Would Jesus Be?" *The New York Times,* September 3, 2016.

Brian D. McLaren. *The Great Spiritual Migration: How the World's Largest Religion Is Seeking a Better Way to Be Christian.* New York: Penguin, 2016.

Montaldo, Jonathan. *A Year with Thomas Merton: Daily Meditations from His Journals.* New York: HarperCollins, 2004.

Merton, Thomas. *The Inner Experience: Notes on Contemplation.* Edited with an Introduction by William H. Shannon. San Francisco: HarperSanFrancisco, 2003.

———. *New Seeds of Contemplation.* New York: New Directions, 1961.

———. *No Man Is an Island.* Boston: Shambala, 1955.

———. "Rain and the Rhinoceros." In *Raids on the Unspeakable,* 9–23. New York: New Directions, 1966.

Suzuki, Shunryu. *Zen Mind, Beginner's Mind.* New York: Weatherhill, 1970.

Underhill, Evelyn. *Practical Mysticism: A Little Book for Normal People & Abba. Meditations Based on the Lord's Prayer.* New York: Vintage Spiritual Classics, 2014. (Originally 1914).

Young, Emma. "Brief Mindfulness Training Does Not Foster Empathy, and Can Even Make Narcissists Worse." *The British Psychological Society Research Digest* 16 3 (2017) 251–69.